OUR UNFINISHED BUSINESS

O·U·R
UNFINISHED
BUSINESS

THE U.S. CATHOLIC
BISHOPS' LETTERS ON PEACE
AND THE ECONOMY

PHILLIP BERRYMAN

PANTHEON BOOKS, NEW YORK

Berryman, Phillip.
Our unfinished business: the U.S. Catholic bishops' letters on peace and the economy.
Includes index.
1.   . 2. Catholic Church. National Conference of Catholic Bishops. Economic justice for all.   3. Nuclear war—Religious aspects—Catholic Church.   4. War—Religious aspects—Catholic Church.   5. Peace—Religious aspects—Catholic Church.   6. Economics—Religious aspects—Catholic Church.   7. Christianity and politics.   8. United States—Politics and government—1981–   9. United States—Economic conditions—1981–   I. Title.
BX1795.A85C39   1989   261.8'5'0973   88-15581
ISBN 0-394-56348-4
ISBN 0-679-73963-7 (pbk.)

Book design by The Sarabande Press
Manufactured in the United States of America
First Edition

CONTENTS

INTRODUCTION

Arthur Schlesinger, Jr.'s, notion that activism and reform recur in United States history in thirty-year cycles is simple and elegant—and attractive to those of us who would like to believe that we are due for another such period. He traces three reform cycles in our century: Progressivism at its outset; the New Deal in the 1930s; and the civil rights, antiwar, and other movements of the 1960s. Each of these was followed by a period of consolidation and then by one of seeming reaction (or at least stasis): the presidencies of Coolidge and Harding in the 1920s, Eisenhower in the 1950s and Reagan in the 1980s.

Interestingly, no uniform economic factor explains these cycles. The New Deal was a response to the Great Depression, while Progressivism and the sixties movements took place in periods of economic expansion. It seems only common sense that a nation cannot sustain continual change and turmoil; it is not surprising that periods of intense activism are followed by periods of consolidation and even apparent reaction, at intervals of roughly a generation in length.

"At some point," says Schlesinger, "shortly before or after the year 1990, there should come a sharp change in the national mood and direction—a change comparable to those bursts of innovation and reform that followed the accessions to office of Theodore Roosevelt in 1901, of Franklin Roosevelt in 1933 and of John Kennedy in 1961. The 1990s should be the turn in the generational succession for the young men and women who came of political age in the Kennedy years."

Such upheavals are not necessarily generated by the presidents associated with them; their presidencies coincide with and are propelled by the exigencies and events of particular periods. In the twilight of Reaganism, there are growing indications that major shifts may be taking place in the public mood. If history is any gauge, the next cycle will not merely reprise the 1960s but will address the new problems the nation has been accumulating over the years when private good was pursued at the cost of public good.

Central to any discussion of a new national agenda are issues connected with the arms race and the direction of the economy. I believe two pastoral letters by the American Catholic bishops, *The Challenge of Peace: God's Promise and Our Response* (1983) and *Economic Justice for All: Catholic Social Teaching and the U.S. Economy* (1986), provide a useful framework for discussing the new national agenda.

I am not the first to admire the elegance and insight of these documents; they have in fact been praised by prominent figures of various political persuasions since they began to circulate publicly. George Kennan, for example, wrote that the peace pastoral "may fairly be described as the most profound and searching inquiry yet conducted by any responsible collective body into the relations of nuclear weaponry, and indeed of modern war in general, to moral philosophy, to politics and to the conscience of the national state." In congressional testimony, Nobel laureate economist Lawrence Klein called the first draft of the letter on the economy a "careful, scholarly assessment" and said that the bishops had "done a great service by raising many questions that have faded into the background in the midst of overall recovery of the economy." At the same hearing, James Tobin, another Nobel laureate, recognized that although the bishops' values were based on Catholic theology, he as "an unrepentant 'secular humanist' " found them "of universal appeal, striking responsive chords among persons of all religious faiths and of none."

While the letters earned high praise from liberals, conservatives were predictably opposed. Writing about the economics pastoral, William F. Buckley, Jr., accused the bishops of "intellectual slovenliness," while George Will said the bishops "hurl clichés," "confuse exhortation with argument," "never entertain a doubt about government programs," and sound "like just another liberal lobby." Shortly before the peace pastoral was issued, Michael Novak, a well-known Catholic neoconservative, issued a kind of counterpastoral. A few months later, armed with $100,000 in corporate money, he and former treasury secretary William Simon organized a set of hearings to issue a "lay letter" on the economy in order to influence the debate around the pastoral letter on the economy then being prepared.

Such criticism and organizing indicates that the bishops were opposing key aspects of the agenda of conservatives, who were then enjoying new respectability, influence, and power. Both letters arose out of decisions made at the November 1980 annual meeting of the bishops in Washington, D.C., convened just as the Reagan era opened. The concerns over a growing danger of nuclear war that would result in Jonathan Schell's *The Fate of the Earth* (1982) and the TV film *The Day After* (1983) were already at work. At that meeting Auxiliary Bishop Thomas Gumbleton of Detroit mentioned the conviction of the just-elected Ronald Reagan that the United States must strive for nuclear superiority and Vice President–elect George Bush's belief that the United States must be prepared to fight and win a nuclear war. Concern over the foreseeable human impact of cuts in social spending and overtly probusiness policies prompted Auxiliary

Bishop Peter Rosazza of Hartford to propose that the bishops produce a statement on capitalism (like the statement they had recently issued on communism).

That bishops should make pronouncements on the arms race or economic issues was not new. Modern "Catholic social teaching" traces back to Pope Leo XIII's 1891 encyclical, *Rerum Novarum,* on labor. Twentieth-century popes have spoken eloquently on the horrors of modern war. These two letters nevertheless stand out for two reasons. First, in contrast to the usual Vatican practice of releasing final documents in a rather oracular manner, the U.S. bishops engaged in an extensive consultation process, holding hearings, releasing three successive drafts, and considering many thousands of pages of written commentary on each letter. Second, the letters were far more specific than most church documents, and their policy recommendations were directly relevant to ongoing debates, even if the bishops did not endorse specific pieces of legislation.

In the peace pastoral, for example, they opposed the quest for nuclear superiority, the development of first-strike weapons, and the lowering of the threshold between nonnuclear and nuclear weapons, and they supported the notion of a "freeze" on the testing, production, and deployment of new nuclear weapons systems by the superpowers. Among the administration's efforts to blunt the criticism was a *Wall Street Journal* article by Navy Secretary John Lehman appearing the day the bishops began their November 1982 meeting to discuss the second draft and a letter from National Security Advisor William Clark to the bishops that was leaked to the *New York Times* during that meeting—before Cardinal Joseph Bernardin, the head of the drafting committee, received his copy.

Published three years later, the letter on the economy did not represent such a direct clash with the administration, but its reading of the economic situation ran quite contrary to the "America-Is-Back" style that Reagan's image setters used effectively in the 1984 reelection campaign. Their consultation process went far beyond the boundaries of the Roman Catholic church. Appearing at one of the bishops' later hearings, John Kenneth Galbraith urged the bishops to hold their ground, while Milton Friedman wrote that the bishops' policy proposals would make matters worse. He added, characteristically, "the collectivist moral strain that pervades the document is repellant."

Just where do these documents fit into the ongoing public debate? Are they religious or political? Who are the bishops trying to influence: policy makers, the general public, or their own flocks? Is their argument grounded in faith or reason? What competence in areas as secular as nuclear weapons and the economy can Catholic bishops claim?

The bishops give these questions a both-and type of answer. While the letter on peace is addressed "principally to the Catholic community," the bishops "want to make a contribution to the wider public debate" (CP, summary; see also EJA, 27). Each letter makes explicit appeal to the Bible and to Christian tradition, but the bishops believe their convictions "are also supported by a long tradition of . . . philosophical reflection and through the reasoned analysis of human experience by contemporary men and women" (EJA, 28). They do not claim technical expertise. "We write as pastors, not public officials. We speak as moral teachers, not economic technicians. We seek not to make some political or ideological point, but to lift up the human and ethical dimensions of economic life, aspects too often neglected in public discussion" (Pastoral Message, 7; cf. also CP, 331).

As noted, these letters provoked unusual discussion while they were in process. Surveying twenty-eight major newspapers during the month after the release of the first draft of the letter on the economy, two academics researchers counted "twenty-two thousand lines of news items, analysis and editorials" devoted to the pastoral. The spice of controversy made the letters newsworthy.

However, I believe *The Challenge of Peace* and *Economic Justice for All* are more than responses to Reaganism. They are valuable resources for formulating the national agenda in the post-Reagan era. The dream of a Reagan revolution, a sea change comparable to the New Deal, was not achieved. Reagan's undeniable populist appeal enabled his administration to halt or reduce federal social spending and to increase military spending, but "big government" remains in place. Under Reagan the United States became a world-class debtor nation—indeed the undisputed champion. Government deficits and trade deficits defy measures to reduce them. The aim of restoring American dominance is only made more pathetic by actions such as the 1983 invasion of Grenada and the 1986 bombing of Libya. Given the backlog of unresolved problems, both domestic and international, the Reagan years may eventually be seen as more an interregnum than a revolution.

Developments in the Soviet Union also provide a context propitious for new directions in U.S. policy. Military spending is constricting the ability of the USSR to modernize its economy and to supply the consumer goods demanded by Soviet citizens. Glasnost has an economic underpinning insofar as modernization seems to demand liberalization, including freer access to information and greater accountability. It is in the real interest of both superpowers to avoid a runaway arms race so as to be able to employ more of their resources in the domestic economy. Although the celebrity mentality of the U.S. media leads them to personalize these developments in Mikhail Gorbachev, he in fact represents the accession of a new generation in Soviet society. Generational shifts in both superpowers may offer the possibility of a new relationship between them.

Eight years of Reaganism have left their mark on the Democrats. Writing in *The Nation*, Alexander Cockburn and Robert Pollin described what they called the "hardhead Democrats," that is, those who in the name of "realism" tend to shift away from their party's traditional compassion for poor and working people. One example of this mentality was a December 1986 document produced by the Democratic Leadership Council, which the media praised as "hardheaded." Contrary to the view of the mainstream media, Cockburn and Pollin preferred the bishops' letter on the economy, which they agreed was not a "blueprint" but nevertheless offered "a sound general philosophic scheme." In a "renewed political culture" it could help open the way to policies that would meet "hardhead" priorities of efficiency and stability "within the utterly unhardhead context of a program that respects human rights and demands social justice." Both letters offer elements of a new orientation at a time when a new administration seeks to shift course.

However, it would be a mistake to see them as simply nudging U.S. policies toward the liberal end of the political spectrum. Although the letters have been taken seriously by economists, political scientists, and politicians and used in university courses, they do not, strictly speaking, offer anything new in the way of policy proposals. They seek to bring the Catholic tradition to bear on critical public issues and, by implication, on longer range cultural trends. The bishops take an explicitly ethical and religious stand and explicate their position both in terms of Christian tradition and in dialogue with, and critique of, major strains of political philosophy. For example, Catholic "communitarianism" provides a basis for human-rights thinking that is alien to both liberals and conservatives. Their contribution lies largely in the fact that they go beyond the bounds of conventional discussions.

Consider, too the fact that the letters are the product of the leadership of the Roman Catholic church, the largest single denomination in the United States, representing approximately one-quarter of all Americans. Certainly there is no reason that Catholics will automatically follow their bishops' lead on social issues: approximately 90 percent of U.S. Catholics dissent from official Church teaching on contraception. Both letters produced some public disagreement in the Catholic community. On the other hand, survey data showed an astounding 22 percent jump in Catholic opposition to nuclear weapons in the year after the issuance of the peace pastoral (1983–84). If taken seriously, *The Challenge of Peace* and *Economic Justice for All* put the Catholic church on the side of forces and groups seeking major changes in U.S. society and policies.

Latin American Catholicism may furnish an instructive example. In a burst of creativity following Vatican Council II (1962–1965), the Church developed new pastoral approaches, especially lay-led base-communities in villages and barrios, and liberation theology, a reinterpretation of Christian faith out of the suffering and struggle of the poor. Documents of the Latin American bishops issuing from meetings in Medellín, Colombia (1968), and Puebla, Mexico (1979), as well as numerous documents by the hierarchies of individual countries have been used as tools by a generation of socially active Catholics. In the process Latin American Catholicism is forging its own distinct identity. Something similar, although less dramatic, may be seen in the U.S. bishops' pastoral letters on peace and nuclear weapons. As I will argue in chapter 1, they may reflect an important stage in the "Americanization" of Roman Catholicism in the United States.

These letters are of more than momentary interest, then, both because of their contribution to public dialogue on the national agenda for the end of the century and because they are a framework for Catholic participation in public life.

Why a book on the pastoral letters? Why not let them speak for themselves? I believe this book can be helpful in several ways. Some matters that the bishops take for granted, such as the nature of "Catholic social teaching," require explanation for the lay (or non-Catholic) reader. A summary of the major critiques of the letters as well as of the historical context of their publication can help clarify just what the bishops did and did not say. Moreover, many readers will raise questions that may not be answered by the bishops themselves or their in-house commentators, such as the seeming contradiction between their liberal stances on peace and the economy and their conservatism in matters of sexual morality and doctrinal authority. Finally, there is considerable value in reading the two letters in tandem so as to draw out their common vision.

My main object, then, is to explicate the content of these two documents and their import for the United States. Of course my own convictions inevitably influence my presentation. Nevertheless, I am not attempting to stretch the bishops' statements in the direction I favor but to present fairly what they say in its complexity.

I wish to thank a number of people for their help. Bishops Thomas Gumbleton (auxiliary of Detroit), Peter Rosazza (auxiliary of Hartford), and George Speltz (retired, Saint Cloud) granted interviews as did Bryan Hehir, David Hollenbach, Mary O'Keefe, and Sister Ann Boniface. A number of others provided helpful suggestions or leads along the way: Eileen Dooley, Mary Hunt, Daniel Maguire, Tom Quigley, Maria Riley, and Nancy Sylvester. Several have read all or portions of the manuscript and offered useful corrections and criticism: Christine Gudorf, David Hollenbach, Ronald Krietemeyer, Francis Meehan, William Murnion, Rodger Van Allen, Joe Walsh. Naturally, none would agree with everything said here, nor should any be held responsible for remaining shortcomings.

Chapter 1 situates the documents in the evolving story of U.S. Catholicism and explains their common method and vision. Chapters 2 and 3 deal with *The Challenge of Peace* and the debates around it. Chapters 4 and 5 take up *Economic Justice for All* in a similar fashion. Chapter 6 asks how such documents relate to the institutional life of the Church. In chapter 7 I raise further questions and point to what I believe are the deeper implications of these letters.

This book, then, is certainly about how to read these two episcopal documents. The larger and more important "reading," however, is not of a text but of our situation in the late twentieth century. The ultimate test of the bishops' documents is not whether they persuade us to see things as they do, but whether they aid us to become more engaged in dealing with the fundamental issues of our time in the quest for a peaceful world where all persons can attain dignity and fulfillment.

OUR UNFINISHED BUSINESS

· 1 ·

A VISION: CATHOLIC AND AMERICAN

In *The Challenge of Peace* the bishops define their task as examining "whether and how our religious-moral tradition can assess, direct, contain and, we hope, help to eliminate the threat posed to the human family by the nuclear arsenals of the world" (122). Similarly, in *Economic Justice for All* their aim is "to make the legacy of Christian social thought a living, growing resource that can inspire hope and help shape the future" (26).

In the central portion of this book (chapters 2 through 5) we will follow in detail how they structure and develop their argument and some of the major critical responses. First, however, it seems useful to examine what the letters have in common: their process and structure and their underlying vision. We should also make some observations on the Catholic church, its American variety, and the bishops themselves.

CATHOLIC RENEWAL

Most of the bishops who wrote, debated, and approved the letters on peace and the economy were priests in their thirties or early forties during Vatican Council II (1962–1965). That turning point in the Roman Catholic church was a major watershed in their own lives as well. Without the renewal process growing out of the Council the letters would have been inconceivable.

Pre–Vatican II Catholicism was the product of centuries of resistance to Protestantism and indeed to all forms of modernity. As recently as 1950 Pope Pius XII in his encyclical *Humani Generis* criticized what was being called *la nouvelle théologie* which sought to engage in dialogue with modern intellectual currents like existentialism. The pope also warned against dangerous scriptural interpretations and ideas incompatible with Catholic doctrine. For example, assuming that the Scriptures teach that the human race has descended from one couple, the pope upheld "monogenism" and declared evolutionary theories positing human descent from more than one couple incompatible with the faith. To see an affinity with the "creationism" of Christian fundamentalists today is not farfetched. In fact, Catholicism was then a kind of papal fundamentalism. Official moral teaching showed a similar rigidity and was quite preoccupied with sexual matters.

Despite official resistance, however, some Catholic scholars in the early and middle decades of this century returned to a Christian tradition older and broader than the Catholicism prevalent since the Catholic Counter-Reformation of the sixteenth century. Vatican II ratified this retrieval of history. Catholics began to read the Bible and to worship in their own languages; the Catholic church formally renounced its yearning for recognition from the state; Christian faith was understood as serving human progress, not hostile to it.

To use a contemporary analogy, the Council era opened up a kind of glasnost, and Catholics began to feel free to raise issues previously off-limits. Similarly, the pastoral changes entailed a kind of perestroika as new kinds of structures such as parish councils and priests' senates were introduced. Although today many might feel that much further change is still required, the immediate postconciliar shifts were dramatic.

Vatican II also took positions on peace and economic questions. In their document "The Church in the Modern World," the bishops condemned indiscriminate war against whole populations, warned against the danger of the arms race, and even praised pacifists. One could see what they said on economic development as essentially the affirmation of a kind of humanism, stressing the continuity between human progress and God's grace in the world in contrast to the otherworldly vision characteristic of Christianity for many centuries.

One institutional result of the Council was the synod of bishops, a forum in which the world's Catholic bishops have met in Rome generally every three years. The theme of the 1971 synod was "Justice in the World." In its most quoted sentence, the bishops called "action on behalf of justice and participation in the transformation of the world" "a constitutive dimension of the preaching of the Gospel." In other words struggling for justice is central—not optional—to the Church's business. In that same passage they spoke of "the Church's mission for the redemption of the human race and its liberation from every oppressive situation." The use of the word *liberation* shows the influence of Latin America and specifically that of a preparatory document by the Peruvian bishops. The 1974 synod, whose topic was evangelization, reaffirmed the "mutual relationship between evangelization and integral salvation or the complete liberation of human beings and of peoples."

Of course these Church documents did not drop out of the heavens. They were a reflection of, and a response to, issues of concern among significant sectors of the Church. In Latin America, the home of a large proportion of the world's Catholics, "liberation" had emerged as a key symbol of people's aspirations; a rapidly emerging liberation theology served as the basis for a new kind of pastoral work with the poor. In a less dramatic way, some American Catholics were experiencing the post–Vatican II renewal as a call to become involved in the struggle for a more just and peaceful world. Catholic protest against the Vietnam War, for example, had a liturgical flair: pouring blood on draft card files. During the 1970s Catholics were repeatedly involved in dramatic actions of civil disobedience. In 1980, for example, Daniel and Philip Berrigan and six others entered a General Electric facility in King of Prussia, Pennsylvania, and bashed away at the nose cones of nuclear delivery systems as a modern way of beating swords into plowshares.

These were of course minority actions. Most Catholics were far from seeing much connection between their faith and worldly matters such as the arms race or economic policy. Nevertheless, significant groups have refocused their work in terms of peace. Catholic sisters, in particular, have increasingly moved away from their traditional classroom role to become involved in social service, community organizing, and advocacy. For example, in 1971 a group of sisters began Network, which describes itself as a "peace and justice lobby." Because Network has members, sisters and others, around the country, it can mobilize a good deal of citizen response to legislation with important ethical-social consequences.

Thus *The Challenge of Peace* and *Economic Justice for All* are best seen as the outgrowth of a process of Catholic renewal, including a commitment to the pursuit of peace and justice, at the level of Church leadership and efforts to carry out that commitment by significant groups of Catholics. However, to understand the letters, we must also consider the particular characteristics of American Catholicism.

CATHOLICISM, AMERICAN-STYLE

Although there were some Catholics in colonial times and one, Charles Carroll, was a signer of the Declaration of Independence, Catholics formed only a tiny proportion of the population until the waves of immigrants in the later nineteenth century. Among the immigrants were Germans, Italians, Poles, and others, but it was the Irish who predominated. In some Catholic dioceses, as many as half the priests were Irish well into the present century (as represented by the relationship between the young American curate, Bing Crosby, and his old Irish pastor, Barry Fitzgerald, in *Going My Way*).

While the Church's pastoral effort was aimed at preserving the faith in an alien land, in fact the Catholic church served as a vehicle for gradual assimilation into the United States. Parish societies and clubs often served as rallying points. Many parishes were specifically ethnic: in the same area there might be a Polish or Lithuanian church alongside the regular parish. The Church committed itself to an extensive Catholic school system in order to preserve the faith. Occasionally there were instances of overt anti-Catholicism; more often, Catholics simply felt that they were a minority in a Protestant country.

During the post–World War II boom many Catholics became assimilated into mainstream American culture: they went to college and moved to the suburbs. During this period Catholic intellectuals criticized what they called ghetto Catholicism and urged that Catholics and Catholic institutions seek excellence and relevance to American society.

The 1960 election of John F. Kennedy was an important symbol of Catholic arrival. However, such was the state of latent suspicion of Catholics that in his campaign Kennedy felt obliged to state clearly that in carrying out his duties he would be independent of Church authorities.

Drawing on existing survey data, Andrew Greeley has traced the dramatic ascent of Catholics as a group. In the second decade of this century, Catholics were only 0.7 as likely to attend college as Protestants. During the 1930–1960 period the rate rose to 0.9, and then to 1.1 in the years between 1960 and 1970. The most recent studies show that "the ratio of Catholic college attendance to Protestant college attendance surged to 1.43." There is a similar rate in the professions. "Catholics are now half again as likely to choose managerial and professional careers as white Protestants."

Schooling level and occupation are reflected in income. American Catholics on the whole make more money than white Methodists, Lutherans, and Baptists, but lag behind Presbyterians and Episcopalians.

These data represent Catholics as a whole. Hispanic Catholics, with the significant exception of Cubans, are largely poor. As a body, however, Catholics in the United States have ridden the post–World War II boom to a remarkable level of prosperity.

For decades Catholics had struggled simply to survive, be successful, and win acceptance in America. At the very moment that acceptance was achieved, the Church was plunged into the turmoil that followed Vatican II. On the one hand it had to adjust to changes in what had seemed immutable tradition. Internal Church issues—dissent over contraception, clerical celibacy, the role of women, and Church authority generally—consumed a great deal of energy. Although Catholic social protest was growing, especially through involvement in the anti–Vietnam War movement, the Church as an institution, and the bishops in particular, were slow to raise critical questions about other American institutions. In the case of the Vietnam War, for example, the U.S. Catholic bishops accepted the government's justification for the war for several years. In 1968 they defended the right of conscientious objection. Only in 1971, when opposition to the war was widespread, did they oppose the war and even then they did so on the grounds of "proportionality": whatever good end the United States might be pursuing was overweighed by the destruction and death being wrought.

Although Catholic peace activists might wonder why it was only after thirty-five years of relatively peaceful coexistence with nuclear weapons that the bishops decided to raise serious questions, the answer is largely to be found in the historical circumstances of American Catholicism. A group still seeking acceptance was not likely to challenge the Cold War consensus internally, let alone publicly.

Not unexpectedly, the bishops themselves reflect much of the process just sketched. Although there is little research on the bishops, one study showed that "64 percent of their fathers did not graduate from high school, and only 12 percent graduated from college." Almost half of the bishops have received all their higher education in seminaries. About 10 percent have earned doctorates in nonecclesiastical fields. A third have studied in Rome and another third have studied at the Catholic University in Washington. The pathway to the episcopacy goes more by way of administrative posts in the Church bureaucracy than through parish ministry.

Eugene Kennedy notes that most of the bishops were born between the two world wars, "a period in which the American Catholic culture was marked both by great achievement and intense and successful insularity from the rest of American life." Public loyalty to the United States and to the papacy was symbolized in the "side-by-side display of the American and papal flags" in Catholic schools. That Catholic culture may be vanishing but "it remains the source of the faith convictions, spiritual ideals, and psychological attitudes of millions of adult Catholics." Kennedy concludes that the bishops reflect well the earlier Catholic culture and are in a good position to lead that culture "into an imaginative reconstruction of itself."

The Challenge of Peace and *Economic Justice for All* have appeared at a particular moment in the history of American Catholicism. They represent an inquiry into the relevance of the Catholic tradition for major questions facing the United States. While Catholics in the United States are now thoroughly part of the American mainstream, they are also bearers of another tradition that to some extent enables them to step to one side and view matters from a different perspective. In other words, the religious and ethical traditions the bishops invoke might provide a kind of "triangulation" useful for taking our bearings.

PROCESS, METHOD, STRUCTURE

There are about 380 Catholic bishops in the United States spread throughout some 178 dioceses (some 115 bishops are auxiliary bishops, and around 80 are retired). Although the National Conference of Catholic Bishops has existed for over seventy years, its present form dates from the 1960s. Every November the bishops meet as a body in Washington, D.C. The two pastoral letters arose out of proposals made at their 1980 annual meeting.

Archbishop (later Cardinal) Joseph Bernardin of Chicago, appointed to head the process on the peace pastoral, deliberately chose as committee members the pacifist Bishop Thomas Gumbleton, auxiliary of Detroit, and Bishop John O'Connor, who had been a Navy chaplain for twenty-seven years and who was soon to be made archbishop of New York and a cardinal. The other members, Bishop Daniel Reilly of Norwich, Connecticut, and Auxiliary Bishop George Fulcher of Columbus, Ohio, were more middle-of-the-road than O'Connor or Gumbleton.

The committee's mandate was to review existing Church teaching on war, peace, and related issues and then to develop a new policy statement that would take into account the "need for a theology of peace in the nuclear age." The bishops gathered a body of consultants and staff, including representatives of religious orders, theologians, and some of their existing staff. Bruce Martin Russett, a Yale political scientist, was engaged as a principal consultant. Starting in July 1981 the committee held hearings and received testimony from about thirty-five experts: current and former high government officials (e.g., Secretary of Defense Caspar Weinberger), theologians and ethicists, peace activists, and so forth. During the process the committee itself met frequently, sometimes even weekly. In June 1982 it produced its first draft, which generated considerable public commentary and led to extensive revision. At their annual meeting in November 1982 the bishops discussed the second draft. A third draft was approved at a specially convened May 1983 meeting.

Perhaps because of its more diffuse nature, the document on the economy proceeded more slowly. A similar five-bishop committee chaired by Archbishop Rembert Weakland of Milwaukee began holding hearings in November 1981, which eventually included more than 150 experts, including economists, current and former government officials, academics, and representatives of business and labor, in addition to Church professionals and theologians. This letter also went through a process of three public drafts.

This process of public consultation and revision contrasts sharply with the oracular style favored by the Vatican and is in fact unprecedented in documents by the Catholic hierarchy. Indeed, one can ask whose voice the letters represent. Those who wish to minimize the authority of the documents portray them as the work of closet-left staff members. That seems unfair to the five bishops on each committee who met constantly over periods of years and to the whole body of bishops who discussed each draft in great detail. The letters are *bishops'* statements, addressed to Catholics and the public; however, the wide consultation and the revision process make them the work of a listening hierarchy.

A side-by-side examination of both documents reveals a similar structure. Each letter opens by establishing the context and posing the questions. There follow sections on the Bible, Christian tradition, modern Catholic social teaching, and public policy in a procedure that moves from general principles to relatively specific applications. Concluding sections consider wider implications and commitments for the Church itself.

CHALLENGE OF PEACE	ECONOMIC JUSTICE FOR ALL

INTRODUCTION

World at a Moment of Crisis	Questions on the Economy
• nature of letter	Problems, Moral Issues
	• nature of letter
	Christian Vision of Economic Life

PRINCIPLES FROM SCRIPTURE AND TRADITION

Peace and the Kingdom (Scripture) (27–55)

Biblical Perspectives (30–60)

Kingdom and History, Moral Choices (56–111)

Ethical Norms for Economic Life (61–126)

• just-war criteria
• value of nonviolence

• citizenship as expression of love
• justice
• human rights
• persons and institutions

POLICY

War and Peace in the Modern World: Problems and Principles (112–99)

Selected Economic Policy Issues (127–294)

• a "new moment"
• deterrence
• policy consequences
• counterpopulation warfare
• no first use
• no new destabilizing systems
• support for negotiations

• unemployment
• poverty
• food and agriculture
• U.S. and developing nations

FURTHER IMPLICATIONS

Shaping a Peaceful World (200–73)

A New American Experiment: Partnership for the Common Good (295–325)

• need for world order
• changing U.S.-USSR relationship
• interdependence

• cooperation within firms
• local and regional cooperation
• economic planning
• international cooperation

CHALLENGE TO THE CHURCH

Pastoral Challenge and Response (274–329)	Commitment to the Future (326–65)
• educational programs, prayer • suggestions for various groups: priests, teachers, parents, youth, military, defense workers, people in science, media, public officials	• conversion, call to holiness • challenges: education, family, Church as economic actor
Concluding Exhortation	The Road Ahead

Methodologically the documents stress the distinction between more general principles, to which the bishops presume all will assent, and policy guidelines, on which they expect some disagreement. As we will note more than once, conservatives have tended to object to the degree of specificity of the letters. From the bishops' viewpoint, however, it was important to venture into specifics in order to show how the principles were relevant. Writing as a philosopher of knowledge, William Murnion has also criticized the principles-to-application methodology. First, he argues that the human mind, even an episcopal mind, does not really work in this deductive fashion. We know the meaning of principles only through the experience of many particular instances; our actual reasoning is a circular process of experience and reflection. He also detects in both letters a failure of nerve insofar as the specific recommendations fall short of the more radical principles they are alleged to embody.

Can the letters be adequately situated as liberal or left-liberal or do they carry their own critique of liberalism as well? We can start to answer that question by considering the theological warrants of the letters.

THEOLOGICAL/BIBLICAL ANCHOR

Both letters provide a Genesis-to-Revelation synthesis of what the Bible says about its topic and each ends with a passage on ultimate fulfillment in the Kingdom of God. The central policy sections, on the other hand, contain virtually no direct biblical references.

This procedure represents a particular option. Classic Catholic "social doctrine," from Pope Leo XIII's *Rerum Novarum* (1891) through John XXIII's *Pacem in Terris*, relied on notions of "natural law" and scholastic philosophy and paid little attention to Scripture. Following the Catholic biblical renewal at midcentury and Vatican II, Catholic social teaching now seeks scriptural foundation. It would have been possible to cite or allude to the Bible throughout the letters, wherever it seemed appropriate. Although less systematic, such a procedure might have made the biblical aspects of the letters more integral to the overall argument. In *The Challenge of Peace*, the biblical sections appear to have been grafted on; the corresponding sections of *Economic Justice for All* on the other hand, fit more coherently into the document as a whole. By segregating the explicitly biblical material in both documents, the authors have no doubt made their overall arguments more acceptable to a secular audience.

Does the Bible actually have anything relevant to say on nuclear weapons or the modern economy? The bishops themselves state that the Scriptures "do not provide us with detailed answers to the specifics of the questions which we face today," but they do "provide us with urgent direction when we look at today's concrete realities" (CP, 55). Any reading inevitably involves interpretation, starting from the choice of texts to be considered and the questions to be asked. Different readers find differing meanings largely because of their concerns. Consider, for example, the differences between the understanding of the Bible as read by Martin Luther King, Jr., and by Jerry Falwell.

Both pastoral letters take a salvation-history approach to their topic, that is, they follow the sequence Creation, Exodus/Covenant, formation of Israel, the prophets, Jesus Christ, the Church, to the final consummation of the Kingdom. This procedure reflects the view of modern scriptural scholarship that biblical revelation must be seen as the unfolding of a history of communities of faith and does not give direct unmediated access to a timeless divine truth.

A central focus is on human dignity and responsibility. Earth is not a testing ground for a future reward; human destiny is involved in the destiny of the cosmos.

Approximately half of the Scripture section of each letter is devoted to the Hebrew Scriptures (Old Testament). Its message is summarized in the economics pastoral:

> Every human person is created as an image of God, and the denial of dignity to a person is a blot on this image. Creation is a gift to all men and women, not to be appropriated for the benefit of a few; its beauty is an object of joy and reverence. The same God who came to the aid of an oppressed people and formed them into a covenant community continues to hear the cries of the oppressed and to create communities which are responsive to God's word. God's love and life are present when people can live in a community of faith and hope. (40)

Use of the present tense underscores the conviction that the ancient texts reveal the deeper meaning of human life and striving. The treatment of the New Testament highlights Jesus' nonviolent way of life and his closeness to the poor. The Church is described as the "community of disciples"; the letter on the economy emphatically reiterates scriptural teachings on wealth and poverty.

CATHOLIC SOCIAL TEACHING

In contrast to the way they confine scriptural references to particular sections, both letters invoke "Catholic social teaching" throughout the text. Although the bishops suggest that this teaching reflects a tradition that extends back to the early Church, for practical purposes Catholic social teaching actually began with

Leo XIII's 1891 encyclical *Rerum Novarum*, which itself was a belated response to the rise of European socialism.

In its classic phase, Church "social doctrine," as it was called, consisted essentially of a few papal encyclicals and also of a number of addresses by Pius XII (1939–1958). Although strictly speaking the dogma of papal infallibility referred only to very infrequent and exceptional occasions, in practice the penumbra of infallibility tended to envelop all papal statements. "Catholic thought" could easily degenerate into exegesis of quasi-oracles from the Vatican.

That situation began to change with John XXIII (1958–1963) whose attitude toward the modern world was more positive and humanistic than that of previous popes. His 1963 encyclical *Pacem in Terris* was well received by secular liberals. In writing the document entitled "The Church in the Modern World" at Vatican II, the bishops themselves took a direct hand in shaping Catholic social thinking, effectively ending papal monopoly. In *Populorum Progressio* (1967) Paul VI focused on Third World development and thereby abandoned the implicit Euro-centrism that had marked previous social doctrine. His *Octogesima Adveniens* (1971) explicitly acknowledged that the diversity of social conditions was such that local Christian communities should respond as they saw fit to their particular situations. There no longer seemed to be a one-size-fits-all Catholic "social doctrine." Statements by national and regional conferences of bishops on social matters were now regarded as part of the Church's social teaching. Notable examples came from Latin America, especially the documents produced by the bishops at Medellín, Colombia (1968), and Puebla, Mexico (1979). The aged French Dominican priest Marie Dominique Chenu, a progressive theologian, seemed to be writing an epitaph for the social teaching in *La "Doctrine Sociale" Comme Idéologie* (1979). However, Pope John Paul II has moved to reassert the papal role in the social doctrine, making many statements in his numerous journeys and issuing several encyclicals, most notably *Laborem Exercens* (*On Human Work*) (1981) and *Sollicitudo rei Socialis* (*On Social Concern*) (1988).

This reassertion of papal authority is part of a larger effort to reassert the authority of the Vatican (treated in chapter 6).

Classic papal social teaching was both a reaction to Marxism and socialism and a criticism of unbridled free-enterprise ideologies, such as Manchester liberalism. Pius XI's *Quadragesimo Anno* (1931) could be seen as sympathetic to a corporatist model of society, and indeed the Vatican was slow to fully recognize the evil of fascist and Nazi ideologies and regimes. Post–World War II Christian Democrat parties often claimed to take their inspiration from the papal encyclicals. Their ideology, sometimes called communitarianism, appeared to be a middle way between capitalism and socialism.

Thus, in its history, Catholic social teaching reveals considerable ambiguity. Does it propose a societal model of its own or is it simply a viewpoint from which to critique existing ideologies and models? What is its foundation: the "natural law" tradition and Thomistic philosophy (pre–Vatican II documents) or a broader Christian tradition reaching back to the Scriptures (more recent documents)? Does it represent some peculiarly Catholic insight into human nature—and if so what is it?—or does it articulate what reasonable, goodwilled people already know?

An indication of its ambiguity is the diversity of interpretations commentators give to Catholic social teaching. The Irish theologian Donal Dorr, for example, finds the hundred years of Catholic social teaching to reveal an increasingly clear "option for the poor." Michael Novak, a Catholic neoconservative, finds the Church largely responsible for the backwardness of Catholic countries and he states that the Catholic church, which was slow to understand and accept democracy, has yet to fully understand the intellectual tradition of liberalism and the capitalist virtues of thrift and enterprise. Hence, in his mind Catholics who flirt with socialism, such as liberation theologians, are actually prolonging Catholicism's precapitalist mentality and anticapitalist bias. From an opposite perspective, the Canadian theologian Gregory Baum finds that in his 1981 encyclical, *Laborem Exercens (On Human Labor)*, Pope John Paul stands in critical dialogue with Marxism.

He criticizes both official Marxism and existing capitalist economies, and his position can be seen as "socialist"—Baum's word, not the pope's—if such socialism is understood as focused on giving priority to the human person and community, is experimental and reformist, and is nondoctrinaire.

Any body of teaching that can provoke such divergent interpretations must be far from univocal. The U.S. bishops—who, incidentally, cite works by Dorr, Novak, and Baum, along with numerous others as explicating the meaning of the "Catholic social teaching"—describe this teaching as "dynamic and growing." It is their intention to make "the legacy of Christian social thought a living, growing resource that can inspire hope and help shape the future" (EJA, 26). Although they make a passing reference to its historical development, they concentrate on its present relevance. Whatever its previous history, the bishops clearly believe this tradition has something vital to contribute to a discussion of directions in the United States. Readers may form their own assessment through the present book.

In their "Pastoral Message," a short summary of the economics pastoral, they list six moral principles as "an overview of the moral vision that we are trying to share":

- Every economic decision and institution must be judged in light of whether it protects or undermines the dignity of the human person.

- Human dignity can be realized and protected only in community.

- All people have a right to participate in the economic life of society.

- All members of society have a special obligation to the poor and vulnerable.

- Human rights are the minimum conditions for life in community.

· Society as a whole, acting through public and private institutions, has the moral responsibility to enhance human dignity and protect human rights. (Message, 13–18)

Just before outlining these principles the bishops insist that they have no "blueprint" for the American economy and that the letter "does not embrace any particular theory of how the economy works nor does it attempt to resolve the disputes between different schools of economic thought." Despite the testimony of many experts and the extensive bibliography on issues of nuclear strategy or welfare policy, for example, the overall enterprise is not aimed at contributing to technical debates as such but at illuminating the moral dimensions of policy.

The seeming blandness of these principles recedes when they are used as criteria for assessing existing policies, institutions, and assumptions. Take, for example, the assertion of a special obligation to the poor. If society is conceived as made up of individuals each pursuing his or her (enlightened) self-interest, and if the role of government and other social institutions is primarily that of eliminating obstacles to that pursuit—a kind of minimum traffic manager role—on what grounds can the nonpoor be said to have a "special obligation to the poor and vulnerable"? Suppose, for example, a situation in which the public schools are decaying for lack of funds and there is no strong constituency since the new urban professionals have no children or send theirs to private schools. Why should they accept a property tax increase that will bring them no benefit? Taken seriously, the "option for the poor" would interject another criterion into the mix.

Similarly, the bishops include "economic rights" among human rights.

As Pope John XXIII declared, all people have a right to life, food, clothing, shelter, rest, medical care, education, and employment. This means that when people are without a chance to earn a living, and must go hungry and homeless, they are being denied basic rights. (Message, 17)

By this account, homeless people sleeping on grates and steel-workers thrust into long-term joblessness are suffering a violation of their human rights, just as surely as are political prisoners under Third World dictators and victims of religious persecution in communist countries. It is by no means clear how economic rights can be incorporated into the prevailing liberal tradition, in which rights are conceived primarily in terms of protecting the individual from the encroachments of government.

Milton Friedman indignantly rejects the bishops' listing of economic rights as though they were on a par with the rights of free speech, religion, and assembly and denounces their "collectivist" moral vision. The bishops, he believes, see the answer in government. He comments,

> People are responsible in their individual capacities and through those organizations that they individually form. An obligation imposed on oneself cannot be discharged by imposing it on someone else. One cannot be compassionate by spending somebody else's money (congressionally speaking).

Friedman may not be entirely wrong when he accuses the bishops of viewing society as an "organismic entity." They indeed see person and community as correlatives and view society as not simply a sum of atomistic individuals. They are clearly convinced that it is meaningful to speak of the responsibilities of a whole society even though they do not fully resolve the theoretical question of how to justify such usage.

FINDING A COMMON MORAL VOCABULARY

When I mentioned that I was beginning a book on the U.S. bishops' letters, a leftist friend was intrigued. He said he thought the Catholic tradition enabled the bishops to, as it were, step outside of habitual American modes of thought. He was not claiming that the bishops are Marxist or socialist but simply that Catholic tradition offers an approach to the meaning of human life and the nature of human society outside normal American discourse.

In this respect there are strong affinities between the two pastoral letters and the questions raised by the work of five scholars, including Robert Bellah, in *Habits of the Heart: Individualism and Commitment in American Life*. Their method—in-depth interview of over two hundred middle-class Americans—made no use of quantitative methods, and the authors were scandalously explicit about their moral purpose: to aid in the transformation of American culture.

One of their most important findings was that Americans have no way of accounting for their behavior except in individualistic terms. This does not mean that in practice people *act* out of sheer selfishness or narrowly conceived self-interest, but simply that they do not have a *language* for expressing any broader view. The authors begin with sketches of four individuals, each of whom typifies a different way of pursuing life goals: a businessman seeking individual success, another man whose ideal is community service, a woman therapist whose focus is mature human relationships, and a political activist. All share a "common moral vocabulary," the "first language" of American individualism. Even those whose goals are more community-oriented have no articulate language to justify their option. The only languages available are "instrumental" ("I do A in order to attain B") or "therapeutic" ("I do it because it feels right"). Thus for all four— and by extension for all of us—there is ultimately "something arbitrary about the goals of a good life."

The authors of *Habits* do not believe that people act only out of selfishness. Indeed, they find many instances of concern for others, even among those who define their life purpose in more individualistic terms. However, they fear that if the language for expressing another conception of life atrophies, the coherence of society itself is in danger. Historically, American self-understanding has been able to draw on both "biblical" and "republican" languages. During the period of the founders, for example, a notion of civic virtue was taken for granted. In the process of transformation from a society of independent small landholders and entrepreneurs to an industrial society dominated by large corporations, the original view has been eclipsed.

In their bibliography the bishops list *Habits of the Heart*, even though it could not have decisively influenced their own work; *Economic Justice for All* was already nearing its final form when *Habits* was published in 1985. Robert Bellah, its best known author, appeared at one of the hearings and has written on the letter and spoken at forums on it. In a companion volume of readings intended to complement *Habits*, the authors include a section from the bishops' letter on the economy.

Despite the obvious difference between a pastoral letter and a work of social theory, both enterprises have much in common. They are exploring the relationship between morality and public life. Both sense that the problems facing the United States are more than technical, that solutions will probably go beyond the bounds of conventional liberalism and conservatism, and that part of the solution may lie in a retrieval of traditions that are in danger of being lost.

· 2 ·

SAYING NO TO NUCLEAR WAR

Nuclear weapons are a fact. While most of us work, relax, or sleep, thousands of our fellow citizens spend their working days alongside them. Poised at military bases, near silos, on planes and submarines, they are ever ready for an order. Thousands more work manufacturing weapons or delivery systems or they transport fissionable material. Other thousands do research in laboratories or universities or develop deployment strategies in think tanks.

Facts aside, for most of us, however, the possibility of nuclear war lurks at the edge of consciousness. How many of us, awakened at night by sirens going for a full minute, have sometimes felt, "Oh God, this is it!"? Is the cynicism or nihilism sometimes observed among young people traceable to a sense that somewhere ahead of them lies a nuclear war they feel powerless to prevent? In *Nuclear Holocausts*, Paul Brians has inventoried an astonishing eight hundred works of fiction dealing with nuclear war published before 1984.

Periodically, the danger we live in breaks through. In 1962 President Kennedy was willing to risk war with the Soviet Union to force Khrushchev to remove missiles from Cuba. In Stanley Kubrick's 1963 film *Dr. Strangelove; or, How I Learned to Stop Worrying and Love the Bomb*, characters like General Jack D. Ripper and an ultimate "Doomsday Machine" weapon ridiculed the absurdity of our nuclear predicament. However, the Indochina war—fought overseas, with conventional weapons—and an era of détente with the USSR took the edge off public concern. Meanwhile, whole new generations of weapons systems came into being.

The Reagan administration's rhetoric about "prevailing" in nuclear war and its seeming intention to develop serious reactivating civilian defense procedures brought the possibility of nuclear war once more into public consciousness and thereby prompted a rejuvenation of the peace movement and especially interest in a nuclear freeze. Aware and anxious to publicize the fact that nuclear war would break down all logistical systems and make medical care for survivors of an initial blast impossible, doctors reactivated Physicians for Social Responsibility and argued that the only relevant medical approach was prevention. Popular scientists like Carl Sagan found a ready audience for their warnings about a nuclear winter that might endanger life for all survivors, victors, vanquished, and bystanders. Jonathan Schell's best-selling *The Fate of the Earth* (1982) expressed this new awareness. Thus the bishops prepared *The Challenge of Peace* in the midst of what they called a "new moment."

> We write this letter because we agree that the world is at a moment of crisis, the effects of which are evident in people's lives. . . . Nuclear war threatens the existence of our planet; this is a more menacing threat than any the world has known. . . . As Americans . . . we have grave human, moral and

political responsibilities to see that a "conscious choice" [Pope John Paul II] is made to save humanity.

In some respects the peace pastoral was not a departure. For decades popes and bishops had made statements on nuclear war, and Catholic theologians and ethicists had discussed the morality of deterrence in specialized publications. The new element was the public nature of the discussion and the intent of the bishops to move from general statements against war to an examination of existing nuclear strategy, doctrine, and proposals.

The context today has shifted somewhat since 1983; the INF accords were signed in 1987 and there are possible cuts in longer range weapons looming. However, SDI (Strategic Defense Initiative—commonly tagged "Star Wars"), which President Reagan first proposed a few weeks before the issuance of the bishops' letter, now absorbs more money than all other military research combined. Sold to the public and Congress as a defensive program that might make nuclear weapons obsolete, SDI threatens to extend the arms race to space, make deterrence even more unstable, and further distort the U.S. economy. Although SDI will remain a research program for years, the tens of thousands of weapons still deployed make nuclear holocaust a real possibility. Hence the argument of *The Challenge of Peace* is as valid today as it was when first published.

A COMPLEX NO

At the end of their letter, after much discussion, the bishops reiterate their major concerns:

Fundamentally, we are saying that the decisions about nuclear weapons are among the most pressing moral questions of our age. While these decisions have obvious military and political aspects, they involve fundamental moral choices. In simple terms, we are saying that good ends (defending one's country, protecting freedom, etc.) cannot justify immoral means (the use of weapons which kill indiscriminately and threaten whole societies). We fear that our world and nation are headed in the wrong direction. . . .

In the words of our Holy Father, we need a "moral about-face." The whole world must summon the moral courage and technical means to say "no" to nuclear conflict; "no" to weapons of mass destruction; "no" to an arms race which robs the poor and the vulnerable; and "no" to the moral danger of a nuclear age which places before humankind indefensible choices of constant terror or surrender. (332–33)

Simply to register a ringing rhetorical no to nuclear war would not require a thirty-eight-thousand-word document. The bishops are striving to speak with moral clarity and yet to reflect the complexity of the discussion. Such an approach leads to various tensions, which continually surface in the document.

First, there were important differences among the bishops themselves. A significant minority are, or have become, pacifists. For pacifists it is plain that war is irreconcilable with the gospel of Jesus Christ; the possibility of nuclear war only makes the original prohibition of Jesus more urgent. Most bishops, however, like the Catholic church generally, continue to utilize the "just war" framework. With such criteria, many come to a position that has been called nuclear pacifism; they hold that some kinds of wars may be acceptable, but in the world as we know it there is no conceivable end that could justify the use of nuclear weapons. Others conclude that in a world in which both powers possess nuclear weapons and make nuclear deterrence central to their defense strategies, just-war principles remain relevant and use of nuclear weapons cannot be absolutely ruled out. The resulting document repeatedly gives evidence of the tensions between these perspectives.

Second, there is the perplexing nature of the nuclear debate. *Ambiguity*, *paradox*, and *dilemma* become overused words. Nuclear deterrence seems to depend on a balance of terror: what prevents nuclear holocaust is the readiness of each superpower to unleash a holocaust. Is it moral to threaten to carry out unimaginable destruction for the sake of any good, including "freedom"?

Third, the letter was prepared during the early years of the Reagan administration. During the process, administration officials met with representatives of the bishops and issued several letters or statements aimed at clarifying and defending administration policy. These officials were perhaps less concerned about the final text than they were about the public perception that the bishops were taking a stand against its nuclear policy and in favor of the Nuclear Freeze movement. Hence in the midst of the November 1982 bishops' meeting, William Clark, Reagan's national security advisor, sent a letter to Cardinal Bernardin, the head of the drafting committee, expressing dismay that the administration's viewpoint had not been "fully considered" in the second draft, which was being discussed at that meeting. The letter was leaked to the *New York Times* before the bishops themselves got copies. (One bishop reportedly asked, "Clark? Isn't he the one who didn't know where Europe was a year ago?" referring to Clark's inability to answer a series of basic questions on international affairs when quizzed during his Senate confirmation hearing.)

As the passage quoted above indicates, the bishops intended to bring a moral perspective to bear on issues of nuclear policy. To do so relevantly, they had to take into account technological developments (such as the trend toward smaller, more accurate weapons), war strategies, and legislative proposals. Only if they did their homework could their ethical observations be taken seriously in public discussion. Although they write more like ethicists than like military or policy specialists, their audience is not that of philosophy or theology journals, but the Catholic community and the general public. Their aim was not to settle issues that specialists continue to debate but to help ordinary Catholics see the connection between their faith and the crucial issues in national policy.

The letter itself is the size of a small book, but the pivotal section is paragraphs 142–99, about one-fifth of the total. This section deals with moral guidelines and particularly with the ethics of deterrence. Although the bishops do not condemn deterrence, they come to a "strictly conditioned moral acceptance" of it and only as a step toward arms reduction. It is in this section that their positions intersect most directly with public policy discussion, particularly in their rejection of "first-strike" weapons, of any first use of nuclear weapons, and of any quest for nuclear superiority.

In its final form the letter has four chapters. After a context-setting introduction, chapter I (par. 5–121) deals with the Scriptures and Catholic tradition, especially the just-war theory. Chapter II almost seems to begin anew, with its stress on the urgency of the "new moment," before going into the core discussion of nuclear ethics and deterrence mentioned above. Chapter III (200–73) deals with longer-range questions, and chapter IV (274–329) proposes implementation of the letter in the Church. The precise language and careful argument create the impression that the pivotal section (142–99) was written first and the rest of the letter added around it. In fact, it seems that an early draft of the letter was similar to what would become that core section, although in fact the final document is the product of extensive revision that took into account thousands of written comments.

The letter, then, is not a straight-line document meant to lead to a single conclusion, but rather a synthesis of various elements that should be taken into account in coming to a moral assessment of U.S. nuclear policy. Had the bishops reached a consensus on a single position, the resulting document would no doubt have been more direct. If they had agreed that deterrence is inherently immoral, for example, they might have simply stated their conviction and devoted most of their effort to proposing ways individual believers and citizens, and the Church itself, could work most effectively to reverse the arms race.

Reading backward from the text, one sees the bishops grappling with the following major questions:

- What light can the Scriptures and Catholic tradition shed on our current crisis?

- What is the morality of the arms race at present?

- What about U.S. targeting strategy and new or proposed weapons systems (MX, cruise)?

- What can be done to reverse the arms race?

- What about the Soviet Union?

- What are the implications for the Church?

NO WARRIOR GOD

After an introductory passage, in which they note that they, too, share the "terror" of the nuclear age and wish to address it, the bishops launch into an extended discussion of the Catholic tradition on peace and war and their own purpose in writing. As noted in chapter II, their primary intended audience is Catholic, but they also address all people of goodwill. Three "signs of the times" are said to influence the letter: the fact that "the world wants peace, the world needs peace" (John Paul II); Vatican II's still valid judgment that the arms race is a great curse and harms the poor; the way the nuclear arms race presents "qualitatively new problems which must be addressed by fresh applications of traditional moral principles" (13). They wish to propose general principles (upon which they assume agreement) and also to make policy applications (upon which they expect some disagreement).

The bishops characterize the "Catholic social tradition" as "a mix of biblical, theological, and philosophical elements which are brought to bear upon the concrete problems of the day" (14). Shortly before, they had noted that the Church's tradition on war and peace reaches "from the Sermon on the Mount to the statements of Pope John Paul II" (7). In this characteristically Catholic style, the Scriptures become themselves part of an overall "tradition," although they are also said to be at the "heart" of and to be the "foundation" of this tradition (14, 27) (in contrast to a Protestant *sola scriptura* approach).

The biblical message can be understood in notoriously different ways, as President Reagan himself demonstrated in December 1981, when he received a delegation from the Vatican's Pontifical Academy of Sciences (a parallel delegation visited Premier Brezhnev, other heads of government and the U.N.). After the group had presented its view that talk of surviving or even winning a nuclear war is unrealistic since any nuclear war would make medical care impossible, Reagan thanked the delegation, reaffirmed his conviction that negotiations must be based on strength, and quoted from the Book of Revelation (16:16–21) describing the end of the world.

The bishops' sober approach contrasts notably with such literalism. First, they note that in the Scriptures themselves the notion of peace involves various dimensions, ranging from relationships between individuals and nations to a "right relationship with God" and "eschatological peace," the full realization of God's designs. The Scriptures were written over a long period of time, reflecting many situations "all different from our own"; they contain "no specific treatise on war and peace" but rather treat how God has intervened in history.

As a moment's recollection of "The Battle Hymn of the Republic" will make clear, the God of Western Christianity, with "His terrible swift sword," is no stranger to war. The bishops do not deny that a warrior god appears in the Hebrew Scriptures, but they insist that this is essentially an image meant to communicate how God defends the people. Other themes in the Scriptures, such as the covenant and the messianic future, further qualify that image. Treatment of the Christian Scriptures (New Testament) begins by noting how some military images are used metaphorically. Although nothing is said explicitly, the authors of the document seem to have in mind the way such biblical images have sometimes been used to provide a biblical rationale for soldiering and militarism. The emphasis on the metaphoric nature of these passages subtly delegitimizes such use of Scripture.

Reviewing the life of Jesus and the Church's relationship to him, the bishops note that in his suffering, life, and ministry "Jesus refused to defend himself with force or with violence." They make no direct argument for pacifism at this point, however.

It is hard to avoid the impression that this section was written separately and added to the central part of the text. It does provide a compendium of scriptural themes and an antidote to the crusader image of God. However, the bishops' primary conclusion seems to be cautionary: the Scriptures "do not provide us with detailed answers to the specifics of the questions which we face today. They do not speak specifically of nuclear war or nuclear weapons, for these were beyond the imagination of the communities in which the scriptures were formed." Rather, the Scriptures provide "urgent direction when we look at today's concrete realities." "Because we have been gifted with God's peace in the risen Christ, we are called to our own peace and to the making of peace in our world." As disciples Christians must look for "ways in which to make the forgiveness, justice and mercy and love of God visible in a world where violence and enmity are too often the norm" (55).

Fundamentalists and literalists of all kinds seem to find a straight line from biblical texts to the modern world, quite unaware, for example, that the very words and concepts they use carry ideological baggage. By contrast, the bishops insist that finding God's will unavoidably involves reading the signs of the times.

JUST-WAR TRADITION AND PACIFISM

The section dealing with tradition (56–121) is more than twice as long as that on Scripture (27–55). In a transitional section the bishops emphasize the tension of living in what theologians have called the "between-times": the kingdom has already been established by God's saving action, but it will be fully achieved only at the end. One example of the tension of living in this "already-but-not-yet" is that "in history, efforts to pursue both peace and justice are at times in tension, and the struggle for justice may threaten certain forms of peace" (60). This refers certainly to nonviolent struggle for justice and may hint at the possible legitimacy of revolutionary violence when all other means to bring justice have failed. Some might find in these words a suggestion that some risk of nuclear war is tolerable in view of the dangers of totalitarian aggression and the destruction of goods even higher than peace, such as freedom.

One of the most disputed aspects of the letter is its treatment of the relationship between the just-war tradition and pacifism. Unquestionably it has been the activity of Catholic pacifists that has prodded consciences within the Church. During the 1980s growing numbers of bishops joined Pax Christi, a Catholic peace organization; by 1988 almost one-quarter of them were members. Yet for centuries the Catholic tradition has been identified with just-war theory, so much so that non-Catholic writers who follow that tradition, such as Paul Ramsey and Michael Walzer, acknowledge their debt to Catholic sources. Until very recently it would have seemed strange to refer to a Catholic "tradition" of nonviolence.

What approach should the bishops take? Would not any sympathy for pacifism disqualify one from participation in the ongoing public discussion? Yet how can the just-war theory's tolerance for violence be reconciled with the clear meaning of the gospel texts? Are not just-war theory and pacifism irreconcilable?

The second draft had spoken of "two legitimate modes of Christian witness on issues of war and peace" and had placed the section on nonviolence ahead of that on just war, thus emphasizing the full legitimacy of Catholic pacifism. In the final version the just-war position, which "has clearly been in possession for the past 1,500 years of Catholic thought" is placed first; however, both just war and nonviolence are called "distinct but interdependent methods of evaluating warfare. They diverge on some specific conclusions, but they share a common presumption against the use of force as a means of settling disputes" (120).

This solution does not satisfy those committed either to pacifism or just-war theory; nevertheless, it was perhaps the most honest way the bishops could deal with the real divisions among themselves and among Catholics and perhaps best expresses the perplexity of many people.

Noting that the Council had recognized the right of countries to self-defense, the bishops repeat that "This is an inalienable obligation," but go on to add that "it is the *how* of defending peace which offers moral options." They see that one may defend peace against aggression both by bearing arms and by refusing to bear arms. The bishops insist that "these two distinct moral responses" have a "complementary relationship, in the sense that both seek to serve the common good" (73–74).

In speaking of two possible approaches, the bishops insist, they are speaking of "options open to individuals. The council and the popes have stated clearly that governments threatened by armed, unjust aggression must defend their people" (75). Shortly afterward, they assert their belief that the attempt to find "non-violent means of fending off aggression and solving conflict best reflects the call of Jesus both to love and to justice" and in the same passage note that "the fact of aggression, oppression and injustice in our world also serves to legitimate the resort to weapons and armed force in defense of justice" (78). It is hard to believe that those two phrases were drafted by the same hand. They seem rather to indicate the disagreement among the bishops themselves. Remember that among the five bishops on the drafting committee were both the pacifist Thomas Gumbleton and longtime Navy chaplain John O'Connor. The letter speaks of the "paradox" of living in our world: Christians must insist that "love is possible and the only real hope for all human relations, and yet accept that force, even deadly force, is sometimes justified, and that nations must provide for their defense."

Next, the bishops outline traditional "just war" or "limited war" doctrine, prefacing it with a reminder that love of enemies is a key test for Christian life and that the possibility of taking even one life should produce "fear and trembling." Fifteen hundred years ago, Saint Augustine provided the rudiments of the just-war theory. Although war arises from ambition, in some instances it can be used, especially to defend the innocent. In that case, say the bishops, summarizing Augustine, "the presumption that we do no harm, even to our enemy, yielded to the command of love understood as the need to restrain an enemy who would injure the innocent" (81).

Those who advocate just wars use their principles first to prevent war and only after that to restrict its horrors by establishing strict criteria for when war may be undertaken (*jus ad bellum*) and the limits to be observed in the conduct of war (*jus in bello*). The letter makes observations on the classic just-war criteria: (a) *just cause* (to protect innocent life, secure basic rights); (b) *declared by competent authority*; (c) *comparative justice* (even a just cause has limits and no state has absolute justice on its side); (d) *right intention* (peace and reconciliation, not unconditional surrender); (e) *last resort* (all peaceful alternatives have been exhausted); (f) *probability of success*; (g) *proportionality* (damage inflicted, and costs incurred must be proportionate to the good expected by taking up arms) (86–89). The bishops' language indicates that they see the just-war doctrine as essentially one of restraint, not of blessing war. The intention is to set limits to what states and rulers might otherwise do.

Although the primary purpose of this section is to set out the terms in order to examine nuclear policy in the light of just-war teaching, there are some interesting observations along the way— for example, the question of who constitutes "competent authority" in a democracy or in situations of revolution and counterrevolution.

The letter discusses *Jus in bello* utilizing the categories of *proportionality* and *discrimination*. Response to aggression must not exceed the nature of the aggression (seemingly preparing the groundwork for the position that nuclear weapons must not be used to repel a conventional attack) and the lives of innocent persons may never be taken directly (population centers as such cannot be targeted). Perplexing questions remain: Where do you draw the line dividing the military and the civilian population?

What about military targets located in civilian areas? "How many deaths of non-combatants are 'tolerable' as the result of indirect attacks?" (109).

At this point the bishops shift from just-war theory to the other strand of tradition, that of nonviolence. From the earliest days some Christians have "understood the Gospel of Jesus to prohibit all killing." The bishops survey examples of such nonviolence from early Church writings, mention Saint Francis, and then move to Dorothy Day and Martin Luther King. They point out that Vatican II urged governments to protect the rights of conscientious objectors and praised those who "renounce the use of violence in the vindication of their rights." They further note that in 1968 (that is, in the midst of the Vietnam War) they themselves had called for legislation to recognize the rights of "selective conscientious objectors."

Once more, just-war criteria and nonviolence are seen as more harmonic than discordant. They "share a common presumption against the use of force as a means of settling disputes"; both are rooted in Christian tradition, each contributing to the kind of full moral vision needed for peace and "each preserving the other from distortion." Indeed, "in an age of technological warfare," nonviolence and just-war analysis "often converge and agree in their opposition to methods of warfare which are in fact indistinguishable from total warfare" (120–21).

SAYING NO TO NUCLEAR WAR

Chapter II, which begins at this point, contains the core of the letter, its judgment on current nuclear policies and deterrence. Noting the similarity between Vatican II's call for a "completely fresh appraisal of war" and statements being made by eminent scientists, the bishops say the task is not simply to repeat what has been said but "to consider anew whether and how our religious-moral tradition can assess, direct, contain, and . . . help to eliminate the threat posed to the human family by the nuclear arsenals of the world" (122).

They remind us of the unique peril of our day. "We can threaten the entire planet." We live "in the midst of a cosmic drama; we possess a power which should never be used, but which might be used if we do not reverse our direction. We live with nuclear weapons knowing we cannot afford to make one serious mistake" (123–24).

One "sign of the times" is an increased public awareness. The system of deterrence in place for forty years is now being questioned. The bishops remind readers that Pope Paul VI called the bombing of Nagasaki and Hiroshima a "butchery of untold magnitude"—a judgment many American Catholics might be shocked to hear from the lips of their pope. Echoing the Vatican, the bishops speak of the arms race as a "danger, an act of aggression against the poor and a folly which does not provide the security it promises." They quote from the findings of the study done by the Pontifical Academy of Sciences, a group of some fifty distinguished scientists and scholars from capitalist, socialist, and Third World countries, many of them presidents of their national academies of science or engineering. Their report to Pope John Paul II, criticized "recent talk about winning or even surviving a nuclear war" (presumably referring to statements by Reagan administration strategists) in terms very like those of Physicians for Social Responsibility. The bishops take a similar position; "the moral task, like the medical, is prevention: as a people, we must refuse to legitimate the idea of nuclear war" (131).

In the next breath, however, they confess that "To say 'no' to nuclear war is both a necessary and a complex task." Noting their own experience in examining weapons systems, military doctrines, and possible outcomes, they admit, "We have consulted people who engage their lives in protest against the existing nuclear strategy of the United States, and we have consulted others who have held or do hold responsibility for this strategy. It has been a sobering and perplexing experience" (132). While the threat of mutual suicide and the consequent psychological damage, especially to young people, and the economic distortion of the arms race is obvious, it is much less obvious how to move in a new direction.

Nuclear strategy and policies produce results that would have been inconceivable to previous generations. "Threats are made which would be suicidal to implement." Each side is at the mercy of what the other perceives as "rational" or "convincing." The political paradox strains morality: "May a nation threaten what it may never do? May it possess what it may never use? Who is involved in the threat each superpower makes: government officials? or military personnel? or the citizenry in whose defense the threat is made?" (137).

Despite their admitted perplexity, the bishops are clear that their role is to set "stringent limits" on military policy.

WEAPONS AND SKEPTICISM

The arguing strategy of *The Challenge of Peace* proceeds from general principles toward specific applications, ultimately coming to a series of assessments of current developments presented at the end of chapter II. Questions are discussed under two general rubrics: *use* of nuclear weapons and *deterrence*. Just-war principles lead the bishops to the brink of declaring any use of nuclear weapons morally intolerable and to expressing at most a grudging acceptance of deterrence.

To understand the import of their position, several aspects of the evolving nuclear debate must be taken into account: technological development, strategic concepts, and existing plans for nuclear war, particularly targeting policies. First, the technology of weapons and their delivery has been changing. Earlier nuclear weapons were large and relatively imprecise and hence seemed aimed at urban centers. Technology has generally evolved toward smaller, more accurate, and thus more "discriminatory" weapons. This might seem to be an improvement insofar as these smaller nuclear weapons can be targeted specifically at military objectives. Some delivery systems can be used for both nuclear and nonnuclear warheads. Thus, whereas previously there was a "fire-break" between conventional and nuclear weapons, they now form a single continuum. Many fear that by lowering the threshold between conventional and nuclear war, such weapons increase the likelihood of nuclear holocaust.

Second, there have been shifts in overall concepts of both war fighting and deterrence. Despite easy slogans—the "mutual assured destruction" of the Eisenhower era as compared with the "flexible" response approach initiated under President Kennedy—such concepts are in fact more complex. Persistent indications that the Reagan administration was making operational plans for "prevailing" in a nuclear war (after many years in which the possession of an adequate deterrent force was considered sufficient) spurred the nuclear debate of the 1980s.

Finally, there is existing nuclear policy, including "targeting" policies. Again, matters are far from clear. Thus the Soviet Union has declared its "no-first-use" policy: it is publicly committed not to use nuclear weapons first. NATO, however, has pointedly refused to declare such a policy and in fact has had tactical nuclear weapons since the 1960s. In the West it is commonly believed that such weapons are needed to deter the Warsaw Pact countries from unleashing their larger conventional forces against Western Europe.

Again, both the United States and the USSR state that they have no intention of developing a "first-strike" capability, that is, a strategic nuclear force capable of destroying the other side's strategic force so thoroughly that its retaliatory capability would be eliminated or reduced to a "tolerable" level. Stable deterrence is based on a conviction that both sides would suffer unacceptable damage if either side attacked the other with nuclear weapons. Yet each has reason to fear that the other side might in fact be developing such a "first-strike" capacity and at some point might be moved or tempted to use it. Hence, there is a distinction between declaratory policy and what might occur in a confrontational crisis.

These are the kinds of complexities the bishops have in mind as they set out to consider present and projected future directions. They ask, in effect, two general questions: could nuclear weapons be used under any conceivable circumstances? and how should deterrence be assessed at present?

Under the heading of the "use" of nuclear weapons they discuss counterpopulation warfare, the question of "first-use" of nuclear weapons, and the possibility of "limited" nuclear war. What they say here on the level of principles is intended to set the stage for a series of assessments on current policies and weapons systems toward the end of chapter II. At the outset they note that certain aspects of both U.S. and Soviet strategies fail to meet the just-war criteria of discrimination and proportionality. They also note that their study of the technical literature and the testimony of government officials have convinced them "of the overwhelming probability that major nuclear exchange would have no limits" (144).

In stating that nuclear weapons may not be used "for the purpose of destroying population centers or other predominantly civilian targets," the letter simply reiterates the just-war principle of noncombatant immunity. Some might be disturbed by their assertion that the principle "applies even to the retaliatory use of weapons striking enemy cities after our own have already been struck." No Christian could "rightfully carry out" orders to kill noncombatants (148). In other words, even if the USSR launched a massive attack against American cities, it would still be immoral for the United States to attack Soviet cities as such.

Next they declare, "We do not perceive any situation in which the deliberate initiation of nuclear warfare, on however restricted a scale, can be morally justified." Here the bishops are thinking most specifically of Western Europe. NATO's tactical nuclear weapons are generally regarded as necessary to deter a Warsaw Pact invasion. If, however, such an attack took place, would using even "small" tactical weapons be justified? Basing their judgment on testimony from expert witnesses, especially former public officials, the bishops come to the conclusion that under the pressures of battle, with the numbers of targets expanding and civilian casualties increasing, "it is improbable that any nuclear war could actually be kept limited." They conclude that "the danger of escalation is so great that it would be morally unjustifiable to initiate nuclear war in any form." The question is not technological, but involves "the weakness and sinfulness of human communities."

They urge that NATO move to adopt a "no first use" policy. Their citation of a widely discussed 1982 *Foreign Affairs* article by McGeorge Bundy, Robert McNamara, George Kennan, and Gerard Smith indicates that they are consciously weighing in on one side of a policy debate. To those who believe such a pledge would make the West vulnerable, they say that the Warsaw Pact forces should be deterred by NATO's "not inconsiderable" forces and by the dangers of escalation from conventional to nuclear war through accident or miscalculation.

Even with counterpopulation and first use ruled out, one can still ask whether some use of nuclear weapons might meet the just-war criteria. The bishops have already indicated that they are very skeptical that any nuclear exchange would remain limited. In taking up the question directly their aim is clearly to undercut the legitimacy of policies that seem to take such a possibility seriously. Their objections now appear in the form of questions: whether leaders would have enough information and be able to make the right decisions under pressure, whether military commanders would be able to remain discriminating in their targets, whether there might not be accidents and computer errors, and whether casualties or even a "limited" exchange would not run into the millions of deaths and entail disastrous long-term effects in the form of "radiation, famine, social fragmentation, and economic dislocation." The burden of proof is on those who argue that limitation is possible. They end this part of the discussion by mentioning the "psychological and political significance of crossing the boundary from the conventional to the nuclear arena in any form" and expressing their hope "that leaders will resist the notion that nuclear conflict can be limited, contained, or won in any traditional sense" (157–161).

Here as elsewhere the letter seems on the brink of declaring that no conceivable use of nuclear weapons in the real world—as opposed, say, to two nuclear-equipped armies in the midst of a vast desert—would meet the test of just-war criteria. The remaining gap, which J. Bryan Hehir, the nonbishop most intimately involved in the letter, has called a "centimeter of ambiguity," exasperates pacifists and others. The failure to reject the nuclear arms race *in toto* seems to take the bite out of the repeated rhetorical attempts to "say 'no.' " A centimeter seems as good as a kilometer; weapons designers and strategic planners can sleep easily. Yet conservative critics charge that the overall thrust of the letter is so restrictive that it irresponsibly undermines the whole rationale for U.S. defense.

In their 1986 letter, *In Defense of Creation: The Nuclear Crisis and a Just Peace*, the United Methodist Council of Bishops left no doubt about their position: "No just cause can warrant the waging of nuclear war or any use of nuclear weapons." Some wish the Catholic bishops had been as decisive; others believe their perplexity is an appropriate response to the many-sidedness of the issues.

DETERRENCE

If any moral use of nuclear weapons seems so unlikely, what about nuclear deterrence, which is "at the heart of the U.S.-Soviet relationship" (162)? Might the bishops be as forthright as their Methodist counterparts, who were later to call deterrence "idolatry"?

The most common justification for deterrence is that it has worked (apparently) for forty years. The assumption is that what restrains the Soviet Union from attacking Europe, for example, is its recognition that NATO has the capability of inflicting "unacceptable" damage. Hence the "paradox of deterrence": what prevents nuclear holocaust is the threat of nuclear holocaust.

Stable deterrence describes a situation in which a sufficient proportion of each side's forces would survive an attack to inflict "unacceptable damage" in retaliation. Throughout the 1960s and 1970s deterrence was essentially stable in this sense. More recently technological developments seem to destabilize deterrence. Weapons vulnerable to attack seem to be intended for "first-strike" use rather than as retaliatory "insurance" intended to deter.

Thus, there are moral paradoxes or dilemmas. Newer, more accurate weapons with smaller payloads seem to be more credibly aimed at military targets and not at population centers, as were earlier deterrent weapons. However, such "improved" deterrence may increase the likelihood of nuclear war.

Again, there are basic moral questions: if the possibility of any morally acceptable use of nuclear weapons is almost negligible, how can any person of conscience have anything to do with them? Moreover, there is the question of intention. In traditional Catholic moral theology sin lies essentially in the will, not in a physical act as such (that is, in the *decision* to commit murder or adultery). Applying this logic to deterrence, if it would be immoral to directly target civilian populations or to attack military targets in such a way that the effect would be essentially the same, how can one justify even the intention involved in deterrence?

However uneasy they might be, it is unlikely that the American bishops would have come to a consensus to condemn deterrence as such. During the period in which the letter was written (1981–1983), their reluctance was further reinforced by a number of statements by Catholic bishops' conferences, especially in Europe. Pope John Paul II himself gave qualified approval to deterrence in June 1982 (quoted below).

The letter comes to a reluctant and conditioned acceptance of nuclear deterrence, insisting that it must be understood as a transitory phase leading to negotiated arms reductions. What is striking is that the bishops themselves do not present a strong argument in favor of deterrence. They point to a range of assessments: for some "the fact that nuclear weapons have not been used since 1945 means that deterrence has worked" both politically and morally; others emphasize the catastrophe that would result from a single failure; others hold that deterrence, far from preventing war, is the driving force of the superpower arms race; still others insist that it is immoral to include direct attacks on civilians in the deterrent (169).

Taking no position themselves, the bishops base their argument largely on existing Church teaching: Vatican II, their own previous statements, and Pope John Paul II. The implication seems to be that despite the element of controversy seized by the media, they are simply reiterating existing Catholic teaching and applying it to the present situation. Of particular importance was their 1976 pastoral letter, *To Live in Christ Jesus*, and the 1979 congressional testimony given by Cardinal John Krol of Philadelphia on behalf of the bishops. Krol's unquestionable conservative credentials made even more emphatic his assertions about "the Catholic dissatisfaction with nuclear deterrence" and the "Catholic demand that the nuclear arms race be reversed."

The bishops were between the first and second drafts of the letter when John Paul II gave an address to the U.N. Second Special Session on Disarmament (actually delivered by the Vatican Secretary of State Cardinal Agostino Casaroli). After discussing the present context and noting that deterrence can be seen as a "balance of terror," the pope made a judgment that the bishops quote and obviously regard as pivotal:

> In current conditions "deterrence" based on balance, certainly not as an end in itself but as a step on the way toward a progressive disarmament, may still be judged morally acceptable. Nonetheless in order to ensure peace, it is indispensable not to be satisfied with this minimum which is always susceptible to the real danger of explosion.

They highlight two "dimensions" in the papal statement: the danger of nuclear war and "the independence and freedom of nations and entire peoples, including the need to protect smaller nations from threats to their independence and integrity." There is a moral duty both to prevent nuclear war "*and* to protect and preserve those key values of justice, freedom and independence which are necessary for personal dignity and national integrity" (174–75).

Critics of the letter have charged that the bishops one-sidedly emphasize the dangers of nuclear war and believe that equal weight should have been the given to defense of these values.

ASSESSING POLICIES AND WEAPONS SYSTEMS

Anchored in the pope's conditional acceptance of deterrence, the bishops make their most specific judgments about existing and proposed nuclear policies under the headings of targeting doctrine and the relationship between deterrence and nuclear war-fighting strategies. Both were issues of contention between the bishops and the Reagan administration.

The bishops note that the administration's statements have clarified that it is not U.S. strategic policy to target the Soviet population as such. In other words, in principle, the United States accepts the criterion of noncombatant immunity. However, they note that

> the U.S. strategic nuclear targeting plan (SIOP—Single Integrated Operational Plan) has identified 60 "military" targets within the city of Moscow alone, and . . . 40,000 "military" targets for nuclear weapons have been identified in the whole of the Soviet Union. (180)

Soviet policy is similar. Administration officials told the bishops that while they hoped any nuclear exchange could be kept limited, "they were prepared to retaliate in a massive way if necessary." These officials further agreed that in any event, if attacks were limited to "military" targets, "the number of deaths in a substantial exchange would be almost indistinguishable from what might occur if civilian centers had been deliberately and directly struck." Stating that civilians are not *directly* targeted is not enough. The question the bishops raise—without answering—is whether the use of nuclear weapons against genuinely military targets would remain *proportionate* to any conceivable good end.

The next question is that of war-fighting strategies. Here the bishops enter the debate on recent and contemplated developments in technology and strategy. Deterrence once assumed that nuclear exchange would almost inevitably become massive and would lead to "mutual assured destruction"; the balance of terror between American and Soviet potential led to a certain stability. Now technological improvements make it possible to pinpoint military targets—technically called counterforce targeting. This may seem to be also a moral improvement because they seem to "protect" civilians, but while acknowledging this laudable aim, the bishops question whether nuclear war is "subject to precise rational and moral limits." The danger is that a strategy that makes the enemy's retaliatory forces more vulnerable actually makes deterrence unstable (sometimes expressed as "use 'em or lose 'em"). They further insist that they do not want to legitimize any extension of deterrence.

Combining these judgments with the papal position, they describe their own position in a pivotal phrase as a "strictly conditioned moral acceptance of nuclear deterrence" (186). They then use the following criteria to make some specific "evaluations":

1 · If nuclear deterrence exists only to prevent the *use* of nuclear weapons by others, then proposals to go beyond this to planning for prolonged periods of repeated nuclear strikes and counter-strikes, or "prevailing" in nuclear war, are not acceptable. . . .

2 · If nuclear deterrence is our goal, "sufficiency" to deter is an adequate strategy; the quest for nuclear superiority must be rejected.

3 · Nuclear deterrence should be used as a step on the way toward progressive disarmament. (188)

Emphasizing their concerns about destabilizing weapons on either side and the dangers of hair-trigger launch-on-warning systems, as well as international nuclear proliferation, the bishops specifically oppose certain existing proposals for deterrence:

1 · The addition of weapons which are likely to be vulnerable to attack, yet also possess a "prompt hard-target kill" capability that threatens to make the other side's retaliatory forces vulnerable. Such weapons may seem to be useful primarily in a first strike. [A footnote refers to the MX and Pershing II missiles as possible examples.]

2 · The willingness to foster strategic planning which seeks a nuclear war-fighting capability that goes beyond the limited function of deterrence. . . .

3 · Proposals which would have the effect of lowering the nuclear threshold and blurring the difference between nuclear and conventional weapons. (190)

Consonant with this acceptance of only a sufficient deterrent and only as a transitory measure, the bishops likewise support "immediate, bilateral, verifiable agreements to halt the testing, production and deployment of new nuclear weapons systems." This is clearly an endorsement of the concept of the "freeze," although not of the existing Nuclear Freeze movement as such. Much discussion swirled around the word *halt*, which was seen as favoring the freeze movement. At one point at Cardinal O'Connor's behest the word *curb* was substituted, in a move that seemed to be a concession to the Reagan administration. At their final meeting, however, the bishops overwhelmingly voted for a restoration of *halt*.

The bishops further urge "negotiated bilateral deep cuts in the arsenals of both superpowers, particularly those weapons systems which have destabilizing characteristics"; support for a "comprehensive test ban treaty"; removal of "short-range nuclear weapons which multiply dangers disproportionate to their deterrent value"; "removal by all parties of nuclear weapons from areas where they are likely to be overrun in the early stages of war, thus forcing rapid and uncontrollable decisions on their use"; strengthening measures to "prevent inadvertent and unauthorized use" of nuclear weapons. These last three recommendations had particular relevance to Europe and NATO.

These more specific recommendations—which the bishops elsewhere note are not to be regarded as having the same authority as their principles—obviously had a political edge. They were an emphatic warning against the general direction of nuclear policy and its enthusiasts in the Reagan camp.

As they conclude chapter II, the bishops are at pains to state that their "lack of unequivocal condemnation of deterrence" should not be used to extend it beyond the limits they set out. Some, including bishops, had urged them to condemn "all aspects of deterrence." As they reiterate their misgivings about deterrence for several paragraphs, they state the need for a

> willingness to open ourselves to the providential care, power and word of God, which call us to recognize our common humanity and the bonds of mutual responsibility which exist in the international community in spite of political differences and nuclear arsenals. (196)

REDUCING THE DANGER OF WAR

The remainder of the letter is devoted to broader proposals for peacemaking, chapter III to policy (200–273) and chapter IV to the role of the Church itself (274–329). Less immediately controversial than the earlier parts, since they did not lead to direct confrontation with the Reagan administration, these sections are nevertheless important for the longer run.

We have already noted how the bishops anchored their own position on deterrence in Pope John Paul II's conditioned tolerance of it. Shortly before that statement was read to the U.N. Special Session on Disarmament, the same pope stood in Coventry Cathedral in England stating that peace "is not just the absence of war" but rather involves "mutual respect and confidence . . . collaboration and binding agreements," and must be built patiently "[l]ike a cathedral." The U.S. bishops take this positive conception of peace as a starting point for observations on reducing the dangers of war and building a more peaceful world. These considerations are prefaced by the "fundamental Catholic principle" that "the globe is inhabited by a single family in which all have the same needs and all have a right to the goods of the earth" (200–202).

The letter urges negotiations to halt the testing, production, and deployment of new nuclear weapons systems and to reduce the numbers of existing arms. While they explicitly refuse to advocate unilateral disarmament, the bishops urge independent initiatives on each side, mentioning some previous successful examples. They further urge "maximum political engagement with governments of potential adversaries, providing for repeated, systematic discussion and negotiation of areas of friction." They also lament the spread of fissionable materials, which undermines the 1968 Nuclear Non-proliferation Treaty, and also the acceleration of conventional arms sales (203–14).

Having advocated a no-first-use policy for NATO, the bishops now raise the question of whether turning away from nuclear deterrence might require larger conventional forces with their concomitant costs. Noting that on this question there is disagreement, they admit only "reluctantly" that some higher costs might have to be paid. They hope, however, that "a significant reduction in numbers of conventional arms and weaponry would go hand in hand with diminishing reliance on nuclear deterrence" and expressly state that they do not want to make "the world safe for conventional war." Finally, they express skepticism about civil defense measures, wondering whether they are intended to "enhance the credibility of the strategic deterrent forces" (215–20).

NONVIOLENCE AGAIN

At this point there is a relatively long (221–30) passage on nonviolence. Borrowing from Gene Sharp and others, the bishops raise the possibility of nonviolent defense of nations, including presumably the United States. The argument is that a well-trained citizenry could defend itself nonviolently even against an armed aggressor. "Citizens would be trained in the techniques of peaceable non-compliance and non-cooperation as a means of hindering an invading force or non-democratic government from imposing its will." Against the argument that such a possibility cannot work, the letter cites the heroic examples of the Danes who refused to turn in Jews to Nazi occupiers and the Norwegians who refused to teach Nazi propaganda in schools. For several paragraphs the bishops outline what would be entailed in "nonviolent popular defense." Here, it should be noted, the model of nonviolence is not primarily that of the individual who for reasons of conscience rejects violence but that of the organized movement resisting evil and pressuring for social change. The bishops also recommend that a designated amount (such as an amount equal to one-tenth of 1 percent) of the military budget be devoted to peace research, and specifically endorse the idea of a U.S. Academy of Peace.

The relative length of this passage, in contrast to many other important debates that the letter mentions only in passing or in highly condensed form, is one indicator of the strength of the pacifist bishops. While just-war "realism" prevails in the text overall, there are points at which it takes on a more visionary character. This passage may prove to be a "sleeper" text if active nonviolence becomes more prominent within American Catholicism.

The bishops reiterate their own recognition of the rights of conscience and specifically of conscientious objectors, including selective conscientious objectors (i.e., those not opposed to all war but to a particular war). To put this position into perspective, it may be noted that of the 3,989 conscientious objectors to World War I only 4 were Catholic. Despite some Catholic pacifism in the 1930s, during World War II the 223 Catholics who claimed conscientious objector status were a tiny fragment of a total of 11,887 conscientious objectors.

INTERDEPENDENCE AND WORLD ORDER

At this point the bishops make a plea for a new kind of world order, a new kind of political entity above the nation-states. Their argument is based on "a theological truth: the unity of the human family." What gives that argument a particular application, however, is their reading of the direction of present history:

> Just as the nation-state was a step in the evolution of government at a time when expanding trade and new weapons technologies made the feudal system inadequate to manage conflicts and provide security, so we are now entering an era of new, global interdependencies requiring global systems of governance to manage the resulting conflicts and ensure our common security. (242)

Worldwide problems such as inflation, trade and payments deficits, competition over resources, hunger, unemployment, environmental dangers, the power of transnational corporations, and the threat of financial collapse as well as war "cannot be remedied by a single nation-state approach" (242). Although they do not speak of "world government," they say that what is missing is a "properly constituted political authority with the capacity to shape our material interdependence in the direction of moral interdependence" (241).

Here the U.S. bishops are obviously running against the tide not only of the Reagan administration but of deep-seated sentiment among the American public. However, they are only echoing what has been a consistent theme in papal teaching during the twentieth century. It is perhaps the worldwide character of Catholicism that enables it to see the limitations of narrow nationalism. The bishops note that modern nation-states arose after the Peace of Westphalia (1648), implying that political forms that begin at a given moment may subsequently cede to others. Catholic teaching "accords a real but relative moral value to sovereign states."

Some paragraphs later (259–73) the letter takes up the broader international context of the arms race. The problems of developing nations are said to rival the East-West competition in human significance. The bishops obviously believe it is important to make the connection between the arms race and the problems of development. They also raise the possibility of converting defense industries to other uses. In several passages the bishops strongly support the United Nations. All these topics are taken up again in *Economic Justice for All*.

THE SOVIET UNION

Any discussion of the arms race in the United States entails some perspective on the Soviet Union. The bishops note that many assume that the Soviet "threat is permanent and that nothing can be done about it except to build and maintain overwhelming or at least countervailing military power" (248).

One senses in the text a desire to challenge this fatalistic view and raise the possibility of change on both commonsense and religious grounds. However, the visionary elements are enveloped in numerous qualifications and observations on the nature of the Soviet system. These passages are largely the result of commentaries on the second draft, which many bishops themselves saw as insufficiently critical of the Soviet Union. They were writing, it should be kept in mind, in the waning years of Leonid Brezhnev, several years before the dawn of glasnost and perestroika. The bishops are at pains to make clear that they do not mean to imply that the two superpowers are somehow on the same level. Thus they note essential differences between Christian teaching and Marxism, citing their 1980 letter on Marxism. They refer to a "Soviet threat" and a "Soviet imperial drive for hegemony" at least in some regions. While the history of the Cold War is open to varying interpretations, Soviet policies in Eastern Europe, Afghanistan, and Poland have left their mark. Our own political system is "not without flaws" and we have not always lived up to our ideals, but the facts "simply do not support the invidious comparisons made at times even in our own society between our way of life, in which most basic human rights are at least recognized even if they are not adequately supported, and those totalitarian and tyrannical regimes in which such rights are either denied or systematically suppressed" (249–51).

Is negotiation with the Soviets possible? Bolstering themselves with the "cold realism" of a long quote from Pope John Paul II, the bishops speak of "objective mutual interests" between the superpowers. They note that many European observers are convinced that détente is possible. They then warn of the "trap of anti-Sovietism" which would fail to recognize the "central danger" of superpower rivalry and the "common interest" both sides have in never using nuclear weapons. Diplomacy requires "not romantic idealism about Soviet intentions and capabilities, but solid realism which recognizes that everyone will lose in a nuclear exchange" (255–57).

Only in the last paragraph do the bishops offer the deepest reasons for broaching the possibility of changed U.S.–USSR relations:

> Soviet behavior in some cases merits the adjective reprehensible, but the Soviet people and their leaders are human beings created in the image and likeness of God. To believe we are condemned in the future only to what has been the past of U.S.-Soviet relations is to underestimate both our human potential for creative diplomacy and God's action in our midst which can open the way to changes we could barely imagine.

The bishops do not intend to foster "illusory ideas," but they warn against the "hardness of heart" that could hinder the "changes needed to make the future different from the past."

PASTORAL OPTIONS

The Challenge of Peace is unquestionably an effort to influence the shape of public debate over nuclear weapons. It is also a call to the Catholic church. Indeed, its ultimate effect may be felt even when some of its policy proposals have been superseded by events.

Taking their cue from Pope John Paul II, the bishops say they want to explore what it means to be "a community of Jesus' disciples in a time when our nation is so heavily armed with nuclear weapons and is engaged in a continuing development of new weapons together with strategies for their use." "[C]onvinced Christians," say the bishops, "are a minority in nearly every country of the world." Their model of the Church seems to be that of a small community of disciples taking "a resolute stand against many commonly accepted axioms of the world." Within history "even the path of persecution and the possibility of martyrdom" are to be regarded as "normal" (275–78). This accent is somewhat surprising given Catholic numbers (one out of four Americans) and the mainstream status they have achieved in recent decades. The stress on the demands of discipleship in the quest for peace stands in an implicit contrast with mere conventional churchgoing. Whereas in earlier chapters the prevailing voice was that of an ethicist or policy analyst, here one feels the presence of peace activists.

The basic operating model of the Church, however, is clearly educational (rather than explicitly activist). As a "high priority" the bishops "urge every diocese and parish to implement balanced and objective education programs to help people at all age levels to understand better the issues of war and peace." The pastoral letter itself should be a "guide and framework." Rejecting the criticism that the Church "should not become involved in politics," the bishops also reiterate their distinction between the principles on which there should be little disagreement and their concrete application (281–83).

Next, they urge reverence for life, making particular application to abortion. Although they recognize that many part ways with them on this issue, they plead "with all who would work to end the scourge of war to begin by defending life at its most defenseless, the life of the unborn." (This "consistent life ethic" or "seamless garment," which became a frequent theme of Cardinal Bernardin and others, will be discussed in chapter 6.)

There follow recommendations on prayer and penance. The bishops encourage Catholics to make the "sign of peace" (the handshake or embrace just prior to communion) "a visible expression of our commitment to work for peace as a Christian community." Similarly, they rehabilitate the peculiarly Catholic custom of Friday abstinence. In the post–Vatican II move away from legalism, the law that for centuries had required Catholics to abstain from meat on Friday was dropped. The bishops here urge voluntary fasting and abstinence. "Every Friday should be a day significantly devoted to prayer, penance and almsgiving for peace" (290–300).

"The arms race presents questions of conscience we may not evade." With this statement, the bishops switch voices and begin to address a number of specific audiences: priests and sisters, educators, parents, and so forth. Before doing so, they state that after four decades of our awareness of nuclear war, "we must shape the climate of opinion which will make it possible for our country to express profound sorrow over the atomic bombing in 1945." Without such sorrow, the bishops see no way to prevent future use of such weapons. Nevertheless, their gingerly expression—why did they themselves not make an emphatic public *nostra culpa?*—indicates that they sensed it would be controversial.

Although the bishops use the second person (i.e., speak to "you"), one may wonder how many lay Catholics will in fact read these passages. They may, however, serve as models for the attitude to be taken taken by priests, sisters, or others in their pastoral activities. The bishops recognize that involvement with peace "may bring difficulties" for those doing pastoral work; parents are encouraged to "discuss issues of justice in the home . . . and strive to help children solve conflicts through nonviolent methods"; youth are urged to choose their work and professions carefully; scientists are exhorted to "pursue concepts as bold and adventuresome in favor of peace as those which in the past have magnified the risks of war."

The longest and most highly nuanced section is that devoted to the military. The bishops have already indicated their respect for the many who serve in the armed forces with integrity and in an exemplary way, even laying down their lives (73). Here they insist they do not intend to "create problems," but they also remind that there are limits to what can be done in war. They seem to question traditional boot-camp training methods. "Dehumanization of a nation's military personnel by dulling their sensibilities and generating hatred toward adversaries in an effort to increase their fighting effectiveness robs them of basic human rights and freedoms degrading them as persons." Similarly they raise questions about the impact of combat on soldiers themselves and their treatment when they return from war, clearly with Vietnam in mind. "It is unconscionable to deprive those veterans of combat whose lives have been severely disrupted or traumatized by their combat experiences of proper psychological and other appropriate treatment and support" (309–17). Here as elsewhere in the document one senses a delicate balancing act, since many Catholics are proud of their military service. Cardinal O'Connor had spent twenty-seven years as a Navy chaplain. On the other hand, the gospel, Catholic tradition, and their own reflection point to the need for a fundamental shift away from nuclear weapons and from militarism itself.

People working in defense industries are encouraged to use the letter to form their own consciences. If they decide in conscience that they can no longer do such work, they should find support in the Catholic community; if they keep working, they should also find support for their own "ongoing evaluation of such work" (381). Bishop Leroy Mathiessen of Amarillo, Texas, had faced this question quite directly, since the Pantex plant, where nuclear warheads are assembled is fifteen miles outside Amarillo. Mathiessen admits that he had paid little heed to the plant until a Catholic employee and his wife came to him with a troubled conscience. In August 1981, in response to the Reagan administration's decision to move ahead with the neutron bomb, he issued a call "stop this madness." In addition to making appeals to the administration and the military, he urged "individuals involved in the production and stockpiling of nuclear bombs to consider what they are doing, to resign from such activities and to seek employment in peaceful pursuits." Few employees actually quit, and Mathiessen's statement aroused controversy. However, twelve other Catholic bishops in Texas issued a statement supporting him.

PEACEMAKING IS NOT OPTIONAL

As they conclude, the bishops reiterate some of their major proposals, in particular the need for a political entity above nations capable of substituting negotiation for war. "As we come to the end of our pastoral letter we boldly propose the beginning of this work" (335).

At their final session the bishops seem to have been concerned that the crux of their message might be lost in nuances and qualifications. They voted overwhelmingly to accept several paragraphs proposed by Archbishop James Hickey of Washington:

> What are we saying? Fundamentally, we are saying that the decisions about nuclear weapons are among the most pressing moral questions of our age. . . . In simple terms, we are saying that good ends (defending one's country, protecting freedom, etc.) cannot justify immoral means (the use of weapons which kill indiscriminately and threaten whole societies). We fear that our world and nation are headed in the wrong direction. . . . In our quest for more and more security, we fear we are actually becoming less and less secure. (332)

In the same passage were words that may turn out to be among the most significant of the letter:

Peacemaking is not an optional commitment. It is a requirement of our faith. We are called to be peacemakers, not by
some movement of the moment, but by our Lord Jesus. The
content and context of our peacemaking is set, not by some
political agenda or ideological program, but by the teaching
of his Church. (333)

In their final words the bishops present what they regard as the
ultimate grounds of the letter, belief "in the bright future and in
a God who wills it for us—not a perfect world but a better one."
For believers, "the risen Christ is the beginning and end of all
things." Respecting our freedom, God "does not solve our problems but sustains us as we take responsibility for his work of
creation and try to shape it in the ways of the kingdom." His grace
will not fail. "We must subordinate the power of the nuclear age
to human control and direct it to human benefit." They close
invoking Revelation's vision of a "new heaven and a new earth"
(337–39).

IRRESPONSIBLE OR TOO TIMID?

In this chapter we will survey a number of reactions to *The Challenge of Peace*, some dating from the period of composition and others in reaction to the final version. We will first look at negative critiques, primarily from conservatives, and then at pacifist and feminist reactions. Such controversies shed light not only on the bishops' text, but more importantly on our situation in a nuclear armed world.

TRADITION ABANDONED?

While a research fellow at the Smithsonian Institution in Washington, D.C., George Weigel wrote *Tranquillitas Ordinis: The Present Failure and Future Promise of American Catholic Thought on War and Peace*. As the title indicates, his quarrel with the bishops goes beyond their letter. Through four hundred pages of text and one hundred fine-print pages of notes he pursues his thesis that since the 1960s the American Catholic church has been abandoning its fifteen-century heritage. Weigel, who was once a seminary professor, sees the 1983 pastoral letter as the product of a longer-range decline.

Painting on a broad canvas, Weigel first establishes the origins of the Augustinian/Thomistic synthesis on just war as the great Catholic "realistic" tradition. He renders *tranquillitas ordinis* (literally "the tranquility of order") as "the peace of public order in dynamic political community." He places particular emphasis, however, on the American contribution to the question of peace, namely its experiment in democratic governance as the best way to attain peace and order within the limitations of the present life. In reaction to those who see the U.S. Catholic "tradition" on peace beginning around 1960, he cites numerous episcopal documents to demonstrate that from colonial times onward Catholics in the United States have perceived and defended the uniqueness of America's contribution to peace.

Weigel's great intellectual hero is the Jesuit John Courtney Murray, whose lifelong work may be seen as that of exploring the positive contributions of the American experience to Catholicism. Vatican II's acceptance of religious freedom, not only as a concession to reality when Catholics were in a minority, but as a good in itself, was largely Murray's work. He also reflected on the applicability of just-war theory even in the nuclear age. In Weigel's view the promising synthesis that Murray was working out has been gradually abandoned since 1960.

Weigel argues that the Catholic church has been led astray by its own pacifist and leftist intelligentsia, who have been influenced not only by ideas but by certain key personalities. Hence at one point he devotes twenty-five pages to portraits of Catholic pacifists: Dorothy Day, Gordon Zahn, Thomas Merton, the Berrigan brothers, and James Douglas. Also influential has been contact with the experience of the Church in Latin America, and thus he devotes a full chapter to the American Catholic debate over Central America. Father J. Bryan Hehir, the major staff person on the drafting committee of *The Challenge of Peace*, also receives a chapter-length portrait. Weigel notes that Hehir commands the bishops' respect for his ability to cut to the heart of issues and outline the choices to be made. His own envy shows through as he says, "he who sets the interpretive framework through which the research is read holds great power over the policy prescriptions. . . . [D]espite the public disclaimers, Hehir's ideas have become the bishops' ideas."

Plainly Weigel is offering his own "interpretive framework" for shifting the present Catholic debate on peace back to its tradition. In his view, the bishops' letter "summed up the abandonment of the heritage that had been underway in the American Church for fifteen years." Weigel encapsulates his proposal under eight themes:

- *Human nature*—a more realistic notion of human behavior, especially sin

- *Peace*—retrieval of the Augustinian *tranquillitas ordinis*, which has been eclipsed by the biblical and eschatological notion of *shalom*

- *Intervention*—a recovery from neo-isolationism

- *Military force*—a willingness to apply just-war theory (e.g., for use against terrorists, guerrilla movements, etc.)

- The *boundaries of political obligation*—the legitimacy of patriotism as opposed to globalism

- The *present international system*—definitions of human rights and understandings of the international economic system

- *America*—the United States cannot pursue peace in the world "if its intellectual and leadership elites remain convinced of the fundamental moral dubiousness of the American experiment and experience"

- The *Soviet Union*—the United States must face up to the true nature of the Soviet Union—not accept the notion of superpower equivalence—and seek its change through "pluralization"

This sketchy list of themes gives some idea of the direction Weigel would like the discussion to take.

Weigel sees the main failure of *The Challenge of Peace* to be its "virtual detachment of the problem of nuclear weapons from the political context in which they are best analyzed, morally and strategically." Taken up by "intellectual currents and emotional passions . . . external to their own tradition," the bishops focus on the weapons themselves. "The notion that sheer physical survival, in either personal or species terms is the highest good to which all other goods must be subordinated is not a theme compatible with Catholic ethics." The fact that the USSR is dealt with so late in the letter reflects the contemporary Catholic debate on war and peace in "its disaffection with the possibilities of the American experiment (What would the country that produced 'Vietnam' do with nuclear weapons?); its anti-anticommunism; and its visceral distaste for the Reagan administration." Failing to give full importance to totalitarianism as the twin evil of our time (alongside the danger of nuclear war), the bishops do not read the signs of the times adequately. Worse, perhaps, they have failed to understand the Catholic tradition on war and peace. Weigel believes he is offering the elements for a future rediscovery and retrieval of that tradition. As one of the twelve moral theologians or ethicists who appeared before the drafting committee, Weigel was able to plead his case directly.

Despite the apparatus of scholarship and the prestige of Oxford University Press, Weigel's book is a polemic from beginning to end. Although he claims to be representing a great centuries-long Catholic tradition, most of the book is devoted to documenting its demise during the last two decades. A good deal of the case is based on hundreds of citations from the liberal Catholic press.

Peter Steinfels, editor of *Commonweal*, decided to check on Weigel's accuracy and was "appalled" at what he found when he checked a series of twenty-five references to the magazine. After showing how "Weigel proceeds like a hanging judge, managing to pass negative sentences even on articles whose main point he does not question" (e.g., criticizing the USSR), Steinfels comes up with a "scorecard" on which only five citations are "unquestionably fair representations," seven are "blatant misrepresentations," while the rest range from "significant misrepresentations" to "fair representations with qualifications."

A jacket blurb from Cardinal O'Connor predicts that those with whom Weigel "fences" will "respond with considerable vigor, but the exchange will unquestionably sharpen both church debate and public debate in the best interest of the issues involved." Curiously the cardinal is commending a book that accuses him and his colleagues of abandoning the Catholic heritage. Could enough bishops be pursuaded by Weigel so as to draw back from their positions? Something similar happened in Latin America beginning in the early 1970s when Roger Vekemans, a Dutch Jesuit, and Bishop Alfonso Lopez Trujillo set up a research center in Bogotá and began to edit a journal. Their purpose was to provide an intellectual platform to counter the liberation theology that had been gaining ground in the Latin American church, greatly spurred by the positions taken by the bishops at a continent-level meeting in Medellín, Colombia, in 1968. Within a few years the themes advanced by Vekemans, Lopez Trujillo, and their associates made headway within the bishops and helped set the parameters of discussion at their next meeting at Puebla, Mexico, in 1979. In their final book-length document the assembled bishops did not fulfill Lopez Trujillo's hopes: there was no condemnation of liberation theology, and some of its themes, such as the "option for the poor," were reaffirmed; on the other hand conservatives scored points with condemnations of Marxism and warnings against clerical involvement in politics.

This analogy serves only to indicate that ideas can contribute to significant shifts in episcopal stances. Presentations such as

Weigel's could serve as intellectual ammunition for a counter-attack within the hierarchy, especially if coupled with a consistent Vatican policy of appointing conservatives to the episcopacy. On the other hand, further developments, especially a changed U.S.–USSR relationship, could render Weigel's arguments obsolete even for conservative diehards.

Finally, there is more than one way to understand tradition. In *The Catholic Peace Tradition* Ronald G. Musto has done a rereading of the whole history of the Church, highlighting manifestations of peacemaking by Christians and Catholics. As a medieval historian, he gives special prominence to the monastic role in combatting feudal militarism. He interprets the element of protest in the poverty movements of the eleventh to the fourteenth centuries as partly a reaction to the violence of the Crusade era. There is no doubt that Musto is retrieving—and to some extent inventing—a tradition. On a doctrinal level, it is unquestionable that just-war theory has been "in possession" for fifteen hundred years, as the bishops say. Although Musto is as personally committed as Weigel, his account is less a polemic than Weigel's. He does not claim that the tradition he explores is the only one, but simply that it exists. Most importantly, it exists in the lives of Christians and Catholics from the earliest ages of the Church to the present. For that reason Musto's reconstruction of a tradition may well outlive Weigel's relentless polemic.

NOVAK'S COUNTERPASTORAL

In mid-1982, as the bishops were about halfway through their process, Michael Novak began a parallel process of consultation and inquiry. In introducing the resulting document, "Moral Clarity in the Nuclear Age," in a special issue of the *National Review*, William F. Buckley went so far as to say that the bishops' letter would ultimately be remembered for having "engendered" Novak's open letter to them.

Novak is the most prominent Catholic convert to neoconservatism. In the 1960s he was a leading lay theologian and philosopher, publicly involved in liberal causes, such as protest against the Vietnam War. In the early 1970s, however, he began a shift away from radical and even liberal positions. By his own account, his discovery of the factor of ethnicity, and of his own Polish roots, was a turning point. In more recent years he has written on the philosophical and theological foundations of capitalism and against liberation theology. He served on the Reagan administration's delegation to the United Nations under Jeane Kirkpatrick and has been a fellow in residence at the American Enterprise Institute. His evolution is not unlike that of Lutherans Richard John Neuhaus and Peter Berger and other Protestants, with whom Novak is linked as a founding member of the Institute for Religion and Democracy.

Novak's arguing strategy is not to confront the bishops textually point by point but rather to parallel the general shape of their argument, even reproducing many of the same headings. The result is more an alternate statement than a refutation. Novak uses the "we" voice and on the magazine's cover is identified as "editor" to indicate that he is speaking for a group. More than sixty conservative Catholics adhered to his statement, including five members of the House of Representatives.

From the outset Novak emphasizes the "lay" nature of his own work. Where the bishops emphasize the distinction between "principles," on which all should agree, and "applications," where there may be legitimate diversity, Novak proposes a three-level distinction between (1) the "life of the spirit"; (2) those areas of the social order related to the Gospels and Catholic social teaching; and (3) the area of "worldly interpretation of social reality and fact . . . and in general, questions of prudential judgment." In the first, the teaching of the bishops and the pope is "clear and supreme"; in the second it is "necessary and fruitful, though more open to ambiguity and error"; while in the third area the focus passes from the bishops and popes to the "concrete moral reasoning of individual Catholics." Novak says he limits himself to this third sphere; by implication, the bishops have overstepped their bounds.

In looking at the Scriptures, Novak finds other points to emphasize, for example the fact "that no one in the New Testament thinks of telling the Roman centurions to give up their military careers—neither Jesus (Matthew 8:5–13), nor John the Baptist (Luke 3:14), nor St. Paul (Acts 22:25)." Elsewhere he notes that "from biblical times, the human race has often been warned that God might will or permit its destruction. . . . The prophecies in the Book of Revelation exceed even the horrors of the twentieth century." Although this is not the literal apocalypticism sometimes invoked by President Reagan, there is a hint of it.

A recurring theme is the need for "reasoned discourse" and "coolheadedness," qualities implicitly lacking in the bishops. In contrast to the bishops' (and Vatican II's) call for a "fresh appraisal" of war, Novak notes that "nuclear weapons have changed our world but have not altered the fundamentals of the Jewish-Christian vision." Where the bishops highlight increased public concern over the nuclear threat, Novak points to "a widespread, well-organized, and well-financed 'peace movement' in several free countries." Precisely because of the economic advance of the last forty years, young people have "unrealistic and utopian" expectations and there is a great danger of history repeating itself if the West seeks to appease communism.

Novak's argument is anchored in the fundamental rightness of Western institutions as counterposed to the nature of the Soviet Union, shaped as it is by its leadership, which is unaccountable to its public, the constraints of Marxism-Leninism, and the Russian culture and xenophobia.

Citing statistics at some length, Novak argues that U.S. (and world) spending on arms and nuclear weapons has shown a relative decline since 1960, while the Soviets have continually increased spending. Social spending far outweighs military spending. It is illusory to believe that a reduction in nuclear forces would make it possible to transfer savings to the poor, since the increased conventional weapons required as a deterrent would actually cost more.

Novak argues that it would be wrong for the United States to forgo a first-strike capability or the use of relatively small tactical weapons. Otherwise, a Soviet conventional offensive, which could be countered only by tactical nuclear weapons, might lead to full-scale war between the USSR and the United States. Fearing such a possibility, the United States might be tempted to withdraw from Europe. The only answer is building up NATO's conventional forces until they are a sufficient deterrent to a conventional Warsaw Pact attack.

Finally, Novak shows himself far less vexed than the bishops on the question of deterrence. Indeed, at one point he declares that "deterrence itself is a form of nonviolence, a legitimate use of force, based upon legitimate authority," an assertion that those committed to nonviolence as a way of life can only find bizarre. The following passage summarizes his position and exemplifies its tone:

> In short, given the nature of the USSR's leadership, its ideology, and its political culture, and recognizing the configuration of its nuclear forces, we see no completely satisfactory position: neither abandonment of the deterrent, nor a deterrent strategy based upon counterforce [targeting specifically military forces, with its danger of hair-trigger response], nor a deterrent based upon countervalue [targeting the enemy's industrial base and thus holding noncombatants hostage]. Among these, we judge the best of the ambiguous but morally good options to reside in a combination of counterforce and countervalue deterrence. . . . In due course, the Soviet Union may learn to prefer ways of peace abroad and ways of liberty at home—in which case, peace among nations may be possible. For this we labor and pray.

While there is no indication that Novak will upstage the bishops, as Buckley predicted, his essay, like Weigel's book, is a quiverful of arguments for Catholics uncomfortable with *The Challenge of Peace*.

PACIFISM AND JUST WAR

One of the truly novel developments of the letter was the recognition of pacifism as part of the Catholic tradition on war and
peace. A significant minority of bishops have embraced pacifism
or are close to it. Yet official Catholic teaching, reiterated by the
pope, has maintained just-war criteria even in our nuclear war.
The editorial resolution to this tension was to present both perspectives as "complementary," while insisting that the pacifist
option was open to individuals, but not to states, which are required to defend their citizens.

As editor of *Worldview* and more recently of *Freedom at Issue*,
James Finn has followed nuclear ethics for years. He believes that
in the pastoral letter the just-war and pacifist traditions "are joined
in such a way that they corrupt each other. The comprehensive
view to which the document aspires leads to a compromise, not
of positions the adherents of either tradition could make, but of
the principles of each tradition." Since, as the bishops themselves
admit, pacifism is not an option for governments, policy recommendations should be made within a just-war framework.
However, in the process of preparing the letter, pacifist bishops
were discussing and voting on "crucial policy options for our
defense structures." Finn does not object to pacifists participating
in the debate. "What is illegitimate and damaging to the integrity
of both traditions is to have pacifists seeming to act within the
just-war tradition while they define its tenets so narrowly as to
strangle it." As an example he points to the bishops' statement
that "As a people, we must refuse to legitimate the idea of nuclear
war. Such a refusal will require not only new ideas and new
vision, but what the Gospel calls conversion of heart." Just-war
principles, he asserts, demand "a critical procedure subject to
reason, and open to discussion and debate in the political arena
in which policy decisions are hammered out." Finn urges that
pacifists and just-war adherents continue to work within their own
frameworks.

A similar critique comes from William V. O'Brien, who insists that there is "no free lunch" in nuclear deterrence: "to profit from a credible nuclear deterrent, a nation must be willing to prepare for and face the serious contingency of nuclear war." O'Brien finds that the bishops fail to define any threat so serious that it would justify use of nuclear weapons. Moreover, their focus on means, that is, weapons, leads to "an overriding conviction . . . that *no* just cause justifies resort to nuclear war because of the unprecendented, open-ended destructive character of such a war," a conviction that pervades the letter. The fact that they nevertheless accept deterrence leads to what he calls a "deterrence-only" posture: although nuclear weapons could never be used against an enemy, they may be possessed for deterrent purposes. O'Brien points out that many "secular strategic experts" also maintain a deterrence-only position. He, by contrast, argues for a "deterrence-plus" position, that is, for one that seeks to argue in some detail for what kind of use of nuclear weapons and what deterrence posture is consistent with just-war thinking.

Whereas the bishops see just-war thinking as intended to limit war—and in the case of nuclear war to almost closing the door (the centimeter again)—O'Brien believes the task of the moralist is to examine in as detailed a fashion as possible just what should be done.

Curiously, the dissatisfactions of Catholic pacifists with the letter almost run parallel to those of unabashed just-war adherents like Finn and O'Brien. Relatively few of the published commentaries on the letter came from pacifists. Committed Catholic peace activists welcomed the letter, but they have not devoted much attention to the text itself. One has the feeling that grass-roots peace activists are grateful for the legitimation provided by the letter but they do not look to it for inspiration. With some exceptions, further discussion in the Church has largely been the work of nonpacifists.

Gordon Zahn, whose pacifism dates back to World War II, when he was one of the few Catholic conscientious objectors, expresses the hope that the letter, "its ambiguities, equivocations, and evasions notwithstanding," will provide the occasion for a "thorough reassessment of the church's teaching on war and peace that will entail a just hearing for pacifism and its critique of just-war theories."

When pressed, Zahn and other Christian pacifists tend to base their convictions on religious grounds. For them Jesus' life and message is utterly clear and can only be understood one way. Despite its fifteen-century prestige, the just-war tradition represents a distortion of Christianity. The ground for pacifism is not simply Jesus' prohibition of violence but a deep conviction about the nature of God. Nonviolence may not always "work" in an immediate sense, but it provides the only ultimate security—a security beside which security from arms is folly.

Zahn rejects the notion that pacifists are indifferent to policy issues. Rather, he insists on "the primacy of religious commitment over national identities and loyalties." His perspective is that of "a Christian *who just happens to be an American* . . . not the other way around." Loyalty to humankind takes precedence over narrow nationalism. While pacifists agree with others on the importance of negotiation, the pacifist places more importance on the parties' confession of their own failures and shortcomings and striving for an atmosphere of mutual interest and reconciliation.

Pacifism, says Zahn, rejects "any suggestion that the state (or government) is somehow above or not bound by the limitations morality imposes upon the individual citizen." The pastoral letter had accepted and even lauded pacifism as a personal option, but argued that states cannot do so and are in fact obliged to defend their citizens. In Zahn's terms pacifism "rejects the notion present by implication in the pastoral that what the Christian is forbidden to do as an individual can become permissible (even *obligatory?*) when it is required by public authority under the guise of national defense." In other words, he is rejecting the Niebuhrian distinction between public and private morality.

Against the implicit charge that pacifism is utopian, Zahn asserts that "In a very real sense there is nothing less realistic than deterrence policies based on such threats and accompanied by the

constant development and production of new and ever more so-
phisticated weapons designed to make those threats credible."
Citing Bishop Carroll Dozier of Memphis, he states that "it is
time to file the just-war theory away in the same drawer that hides
the flat-earth theory and the theories about the sun racing around
the earth."

While welcoming the bishops' acceptance of conscientious objection, he says that what is really needed is a "more active pro-
motion of that option for Catholics." His overall judgment of the
pastoral is that "to the extent that it seems to restore the preeminence of the just-war theory, it stumbles and falls short of the
prophetic leadership the church and world need at this critical
'new moment' in time."

A more radical criticism of the letter on this point comes from
Quentin Quesnell, who asserts that the bishops' hermeneutical
method prevents them from acknowledging the central place of
nonviolence in the New Testament (Sermon on the Mount and
elsewhere). If those texts "cannot safely be used in a pastoral,
then no text of Scripture can ever be used in a Christian teaching,"
not those referring to the authority of the apostles nor to divorce
nor to the eucharist. "The problem is not one of clarity or historical reliability. The problem is one of prior decisions as to what
the texts can be allowed to mean and what effect in life that
meaning will be allowed to have."

At that point he acknowledges that such texts cannot be made
law. "They are challenges, invitations, messages of eternal life to
all who hear and believe." Although they are "gospel . . . they
cannot be imposed on anyone. They must be proposed to everyone." He suggests that the bishops could have written another
kind of pastoral letter, one that would not have finessed the sharp-
ness of the gospel. "The new pastoral would be deliberately di-
rected to individuals, even as the Gospel challenges themselves
are." It would also look concretely at our world. "The decision
for Catholics reading the pastoral is not whether nuclear wars
shall be begun or what targets the Pentagon will pick out. The
actual decision for Catholics will be whether to cooperate with

the actions being taken in their name by their democratically elected government." Such decisions would range from voting to serving in the military to working in defense or paying taxes. This is still individual morality, but it can sway nations. An intriguing suggestion is that the bishops urge Catholics to support legislation making possible "financial conscientious objection." "It is after all perfectly logical: If 20-year-olds can apply for alternative service outside the military for the sake of conscience, why should the 40- to 60-year-olds not be able to put their tax money to alternative purposes outside the government's war program in order to spare their consciences too?"

Quesnell is demanding forthrightness: just-war morality should no more be equated with the gospel than is a comfortable middle-class life—his own and most of his readers'—to be equated with Jesus' challenge to sell one's goods and give the proceeds to the poor.

Another theologian, Francis X. Meehan, believes that the letter should be seen as a step in a "development of doctrine." He is at pains to insist that nonviolence in the Scriptures should not be seen in a fundamentalistic way. The kind of nonviolence practiced by Gandhi and Martin Luther King is not motivated by a concern for one's own purity but by a concern for effectiveness in history. In a time when "realism" is invoked to justify preparation for nuclear war, nonviolence may turn out to be the more authentic realism.

ANOTHER LOGIC—FEMINIST EXPERIENCE

Among the consultants to the committee drafting *The Challenge of Peace*, the only woman was Juliana Casey, who represented Catholic sisters. During the two years of hearings from dozens of expert witnesses, only three women, a Scripture scholar and two peace activists, spoke to the committee.

> In all of our meetings with departments of the government, the only other women I ever saw were receptionists, secre-

taries, and cleaning women. I often felt lonely and alienated. I slowly began to realize that this was not simply because I was "the only woman," but rather because as the only woman, I was very much alone in a world view, a relationship to reality. Sexism is an evil. Nowhere is it more evil than in making of war.

She reflects on the blatant sexism in scenes from a weapons convention: "a woman dressed in cowboy hat, shorts, and a fringed leather halter top, running a roulette wheel for the enjoyment of prospective purchasers of weapons" and two women in bikinis, one straddling a missile and the other reclining on it.

The image of women adorning death machines and of men ogling both weapons and women evokes something ugly and shameful in all of us. It also speaks more eloquently than any words about what is so degrading in a male-dominated world galloping toward death. Women and weapons are sexy. They are desireable objects which men seek to own, possess, overcome. Little wonder most women feel an instinctive revulsion towards weapons; their "instinct" in many ways is one of self-preservation.

Casey's own book, *Where Is God Now? Nuclear Terror, Feminism and the Search for God,* is not a feminist critique of the bishops' letter—at least not directly. It is rather the reflection of a woman closely involved with the bishops' project, who nevertheless obviously felt some distance from it.

Her book explores dimensions of nuclear weapons that receive passing attention at best in the peace pastoral. On the other hand, she spends no time discussing deterrence, nor does she join the just-war/pacifism debate.

Her first two chapters are a quick review of some basic facts about the destructiveness of nuclear weapons, their costs, the history of the arms race, and so forth. In dealing with costs, she devotes some attention to the "psychological costs," which the bishops mention only fleetingly. In chapters 3 and 4 she looks at patterns of human acting, first "patterns that make for war" followed by "new patterns." Such patterns are considered under the rubrics of language, logic, power, and relationship.

For example, she notes the "male bias" of nuclear language, as in the dread of becoming "impotent" in the face of the Soviet threat, of being "emasculated." It is men who are frightened by a "window of vulnerability." Similarly, male distrust of emotions is at work in dismissing the peace movement as "hysterical." She notes how the "male mistrust of emotions" affected the pastoral letter. In draft form, the bishops described their consultations as "a sobering, perplexing, and, at times, frightening experience." However, the word *frightening* was removed, "even though the experience was indeed a fearsome one for many." She sees the fact that the bishops found it "natural" to drop the term as a telling indication that they share the male ethos.

After reviewing patriarchal language, logic, power, and relationship, she turns to new patterns—feminist patterns. Her examples are of women in action, such as the Argentine "Mothers of the Plaza de Mayo," who nonviolently defied the military who had murdered tens of thousands of civilians under the pretext of counterinsurgency. After presenting numerous examples from feminist studies and from her own experience connected with the bishops' letters, she summarizes "a strikingly different world view from that proposed in the 'real' male-dominated world."

> Language is inclusive, imaginative and celebratory of the feminine. Logic is expanded beyond the limited (and dangerous) horizon of abstract, objective rationality to include creation, imagination and vision. Power is not domination, control, power-over, but rather energy which grows in relation, which enables and empowers others. Relationship is fundamental to development, enables caring, and dissipates the need for enemies.

Since Casey's book is not a committee product and not aimed expressly at the policy debate, it should not be directly compared with *The Challenge of Peace*. However, the very fact that she took a rather different tack may serve to indicate aspects that are under-developed in the bishops' letter, an underdevelopment traceable to the male culture that is part and parcel of the Catholic ecclesiastical system. Unlike the critiques previously examined, a feminist viewpoint finds the bishops wanting not so much on particular issues, but on the unexamined underlying ethos.

Put another way, there are important psychological, cultural— and spiritual—aspects of war and peace that *The Challenge of Peace* leaves quite undeveloped.

· 4 ·

TOWARD A NEW AMERICAN EXPERIMENT

A uxiliary Bishop Peter Rosazza of Hartford, whose motion at the 1980 bishops' meeting initiated what became *Economic Justice for All,* says it was two French priests, classmates of his, who started him thinking. They wondered why the bishops had gone through the trouble of writing a pastoral letter on Marxism (1980)—hardly a burning pastoral issue in the United States. Why not a letter on capitalism?

It made sense to Rosazza, whose goatee and unselfconscious manner do not fit stereotypes of bishops. He seems to be most fulfilled as a pastor, especially with Latinos. Rosazza has walked on picket lines and played an active role in the Naugatuck Valley Project, a coalition that was instrumental in the worker buyout of the Bridgeport Brass Company and is struggling to maintain the region's economic base.

Rosazza's proposal of a letter on capitalism, approved at the bishops' November 1980 meeting, was modified in the early stages as the committee decided to focus on the existing U.S. economy rather than on capitalism as a system.

During the period between the committee's first formal meeting with consultants in November 1981 and the publication of the letter in November 1986, the economy was on many people's minds. In the early eighties the Sunbelt was booming and the Frostbelt (or Rustbelt) seemed doomed to decay. Detroit workers loaded up their belongings and headed for Houston. Within a few years, however, parts of the Northeast had turned around—though not for Detroit's auto workers or Pittsburgh's steel workers—while much of the Sunbelt (Texas, Louisiana, Oklahoma) was in recession. Meanwhile the Reagan administration engaged in the largest military expansion in peacetime history, partly at the expense of social programs but primarily by running record deficits. In 1982 Mexico could not meet its loan payments, and thereafter the specter of a cataclysmic worldwide financial crisis haunted bankers. High interest rates and low farm prices drove many farmers into bankruptcy. It was a time of high unemployment (over 8 percent, moving down to 6 percent around the publication date). The homeless, seeking warmth on subway grates, became an undeniable feature of American life.

Yet the post-1982 period was declared a "recovery." Walter Mondale and Geraldine Ferraro, running largely on economic issues, lost forty-nine states in the 1984 election. Young college graduates marched by droves straight to Wall Street, and stretch limos became a common sight. For several years liberal economists looked old alongside a new group of challengers, such as George Gilder and whiz kids like David Stockman, Reagan's budget manager.

In their opening words the bishops take a somewhat unfashionable stance by insisting that economic systems and theories should be subjected to noneconomic criteria:

> Every perspective on economic life that is human, moral, and Christian must be shaped by three questions: What does

the economy do *for* people? What does it do *to* people? And how do people *participate* in it? (1)

The bishops are implicitly asserting that the U.S. economy—or any economy—should not be regarded as a given, like the weather. It is rather "a human reality: men and women working together to develop and care for the whole of God's creation" (1). The implicit argument, developed throughout the letter, is that to the extent that the economy does not serve the true welfare of all people, it can and should be changed by conscious human action.

Invoking Vatican II's often quoted statement that the Church shares "joys and hopes, the griefs and anxieties of the people of this age, especially those who are poor or in any way afflicted," the bishops devote most of chapter I to an examination of areas of concern in the U.S. economy. They see "failures—some of them massive and ugly":

- Poor and homeless people sleep in community shelters and in our church basements; the hungry line up in soup lines.

- Unemployment gnaws at the self-respect of both middle-aged persons who have lost jobs and the young who cannot find them.

- Hardworking men and women wonder if the system of enterprise that helped them yesterday might destroy their jobs and their communities tomorrow.

- Families confront major new challenges. . . .

- Farmers face the loss of their land and way of life. . . .

- *And beyond our own shores, the reality of 800 million people living in absolute poverty and 450 million malnourished or facing starvation casts an ominous shadow over all these hopes and problems at home.* (3; emphasis in original)

These snapshots are quite different from the nostalgic imagery used during the 1984 Reagan reelection campaign in techniques that owed more to fast-food advertising than to reasoned discourse. The bishops also point to signs of hope: the efforts of parents balancing work and family life, conscientious business people confronting hard choices, young people making vocational decisions, workers showing solidarity, and new immigrants struggling bravely (2).

The remainder of chapter I sets the agenda for the letter as a whole. The bishops say, "we want to add our voice to the public debate about the directions in which the U.S. economy should be moving" (27). Their description of the present state of the economy is something of a balancing act: the U.S. economy has provided "an unprecedented standard of living for most of its people," but the "American experiment . . . has involved serious conflict and suffering"; the "U.S. value system emphasizes "economic freedom," but it also recognizes "that the market is limited by fundamental human rights" (6–7).

As the bishops rapidly survey economic conditions, they first focus on the interdependent nature of the world economy, including the common ecological environment of the earth. They then cite statistics on unemployment and poverty, note the effects on family life, and explicitly connect this pastoral letter to *The Challenge of Peace* by pointing to the investment of human creativity and resources (a $300 billion defense budget) in weapons and strategies. When their contributions to security, peace, and justice are questionable, "spending priorities should be redirected to more pressing social needs" (20).

In choosing to deal with certain topics the bishops inevitably have to overlook others. They here list some developments that demand "careful analysis" even though they are not directly taken into account in the letter:

> the movement of many industries from the Snowbelt to the
> Sunbelt, the federal deficit and interest rates, corporate merg-
> ers and takeovers, the effects of new technologies such as

robotics and information systems in U.S. industry, immigration policy, growing international traffic in drugs, and the trade imbalance. (21)

None of these are major themes in the letter itself. To the bishops they are "symptoms of more fundamental currents," such as "the struggle to find meaning and value in human work," which are "cultural and moral in content." The challenges facing the economy "call for sustained reflection on the values that guide economic choices and are embodied in economic institutions." The pastoral letter is understood as a contribution for overcoming the "split" between faith and daily life deplored by Vatican II (21).

Noting the fragmentation introduced into contemporary life by specialization, they say they hope to contribute to the development of a "common ground." A few paragraphs earlier, referring to Abraham Lincoln's Gettysburg address, they have stated, "There is unfinished business in the American experiment in freedom and justice for all" (9). A footnote reference to *Habits of the Heart* is a further indication of their sympathies. They hope to contribute to the quest for a common vision and language.

BIBLICAL OPTION FOR THE POOR

Having broached some of their major concerns and hinted at policy areas, the bishops open their "Christian Vision of Economic Life" (chapter II) with an assertion of the "sacredness" of human beings. *"The dignity of the human person, realized in community with others, is the criterion against which all aspects of economic life must be measured"* (28). That statement deliberately emphasizes that human beings are to be understood—ultimately—not as isolated individuals, but as persons-in-community. Human beings are ends to be served, not means to be exploited. We should deal with each other "with the sense of awe that arises in the presence of something holy and sacred," for we human beings are "created in the image of God." This religious conviction is the anchoring point for the critique that runs through the letter. "Wherever our economic arrangements fail to conform to the demands of human dignity lived in community, they must be questioned and transformed" (28). (*Arrangements* is perhaps intended as a more neutral term than *structures*.)

As in the peace pastoral, this section is divided into a biblical and a philosophical/historical reflection. We have already noted that both letters utilize the Bible in a similar fashion, providing a Genesis-to-Revelation panorama highlighting human dignity and responsibility. Whereas the scriptural sections of the peace pastoral were largely devoted to relativizing militaristic images of God, this letter draws out certain biblical themes related to economic life. Catholics are seen as reading the Scriptures alongside other churches, and alongside "our Jewish brothers and sisters." Indeed, the bishops speak of the "Hebrew Scriptures" rather than the "Old Testament," a term that suggests that the Hebrew Bible functioned primarily to prepare for the New Testament.

The "focal points of Israel's faith—creation, covenant, and community" are taken to be a starting point. Without emphasizing any naive Adam-and-Eve imagery, the bishops anchor their vision in a "theology of creation." Creation is seen not so much as an initial act but as a relationship between God and people. "Fruitful harvests, bountiful flocks, a loving family, are God's blessings on those who heed God's word. . . . God is present to creation, and creative engagement with God's handiwork is itself reverence for God" (31). This sketch of creation theology concludes with a reminder that throughout its history, *"the Church has affirmed that misuse of the world's resources or appropriation of them by a minority of the world's population betrays the gift of creation since 'whatever belongs to God belongs to all' "* (34; emphasis in original).

All human beings have *"an inalienable dignity . . . prior to any division into races or nations and prior to human labor and human achievement"* (emphasis in original). Treating Genesis 1–11 (Adam and Eve, Cain and Abel, Babel) as a unit, the bishops reflect on a history of sin and idolatry, noting that this includes "not only the worship of idols, but also manifestations of idolatry, such as the quest for unrestrained power and the desire for great wealth" (33).

It is perhaps noteworthy that the treatment of Israel does not single out the Exodus event—as is common in Latin American liberation theology, for example—but rather focuses on Israel's covenant with God and its expression in laws to protect human life and especially that of the "vulnerable members of the community, widows, orphans, the poor and strangers in the land." Expressly mentioned is the jubilee year, in which "property was restored to its original owners." These scriptural considerations lead to a generalization: "Being free and being a co-responsible community are God's intentions for us" (36).

Again unlike liberation theologians, the bishops do not make the prophets a major theme. They do, however, devote considerable attention to the biblical notion of justice, which is "more comprehensive than subsequent philosophical definitions. It is not concerned with a strict definition of rights and duties, but with the rightness of the human condition before God and within society" (39). Since much of the letter appeals to a more philosophically grounded "natural law" tradition, this statement hints that, when taken seriously, the Bible is more radical than the explicit principles and proposals of the bishops. In chapter 1 (page 15) we have already quoted the bishops' summary of a biblical vision of economic justice.

There follow four paragraphs devoted specifically to Jesus' life and message. The commandment to love one's neighbor as oneself and the stories of the Samaritan and the last judgment are given prominence. As in the peace pastoral, there is a strong stress on discipleship: Jesus calls individuals to be disciples today as he called his first followers, and the Church is to be "a community of disciples" (John Paul II).

Half of the section on the Christian Scriptures is devoted to issues of poverty, wealth, and discipleship. Jesus lived as a poor man, blessed the poor, and warned about wealth. The rich are "wise in their own eyes and are prone to apostasy and idolatry

. . . as well as to violence and oppression." Not blinded by wealth, "the poor can be open to God's presence."

There is clearly a tension, not only in this text but in the Scriptures and Catholic tradition. If wealth is a danger and poverty an ideal, why be concerned to change things? Historically, "God's will" has certainly served as an underlying justification for inequality. The response is a distinction between the kind of misery that dehumanizes and a simplicity or austerity that enables one to be open to others and to God. Such a distinction is implied in the bishops' assertion that "early Christianity saw the poor as an object of God's special love, but it neither canonized material poverty nor accepted deprivation as an inevitable fact of life" (51). The description of the early Christians in Jerusalem as holding "all things in common" is understood to refer not only to the sharing of material possessions "but more fundamentally, friendship and mutual concern among all its members. . . . While recognizing the dangers of wealth, the early Church proposed the proper use of possessions to alleviate need and suffering rather than universal dispossession" (52).

At the end of this section the bishops point out that "Jesus takes the side of those most in need, physically and spiritually." This example poses "challenges to the contemporary church."

> It imposes a prophetic mandate to speak for those who have no one to speak for them, to be a defender of the defenseless, who in biblical terms are the poor. It also demands a compassionate vision that enables the Church to see things from the side of the poor and powerless and to assess lifestyle, policies, and social institutions in terms of their impact on the poor. (52)

The Church is enjoined to help people "experience the liberating power of God in their own lives." Jesus' example calls for "an emptying of self, both individually and corporately" (52).

The "already-and-not-yet" dimension mentioned in the peace pastoral is here described as the "tension between promise and fulfillment."

> Although the ultimate realization of God's plan lies in the future, Christians in union with all people of good will are summoned to shape history in the image of God's creative design, and in response to the reign of God proclaimed and embodied by Jesus. (53)

This section ends with a few paragraphs that seek to bridge the experience of the Church from biblical times to the present. It is perhaps surprising that a Church that so stresses tradition should pass over history so hastily: the letter mentions the writings of the Church fathers on wealth, the contributions of monks and mendicant orders, the Church's networks of hospitals, orphanages, and schools, and the encyclicals of the modern popes. The bishops do not ask to what extent Catholicism has impeded the quest for justice and human development. However, they note that Catholics can learn from the Protestant experience, and especially from "our fellow Catholics in developing countries [who] have much to teach us about the Christian response to an ever more interdependent world" (59).

ETHICAL NORMS

Some believers think scriptural texts tell us directly what must be done today. Both pacifists and conservative fundamentalists tend to ground their options immediately in scriptural injunctions. It is characteristically "Catholic," however, to make explicit appeal to reason, not just to Scripture. Indeed, until Vatican II, Catholic "social teaching" was largely based on "natural law" arguments, with little direct appeal to Scripture. In the peace pastoral the bishops explicitly pointed to the limits of Scripture with regard to what to do about nuclear weapons.

In the remainder of chapter II the bishops spell out the principles they believe should underlie an approach to the economy. To some extent, their statements seem overlapping or repetitious. It might be helpful to visualize the structure of the argument:

NORMS (61–95)	• Duties of Life in Community (63–78): love and solidarity; justice and participation; overcoming marginalization and powerlessness
	• Human Rights (79–84): civil and political, economic and social
	• Moral Priorities for the Nation (85–95)
PERSONS AND INSTITUTIONS (96–126)	• Working People and Labor Unions (102–109)
	• Owners and Managers (110–118)
	• Citizens and Government (119–24)

These considerations lay the groundwork for the more specific policy discussion of chapter III (organized around the themes of work, poverty, agriculture, and the international economy). A simpler version of these principles is that prepared by the bishops themselves in the "Message" that accompanied the pastoral letter (cf. pages 18–19, above).

Chapter II does not proceed in a rigid linear path toward a particular conclusion. Rather it explores a given set of themes from different perspectives. To take an obvious example, the bishops consider the claims of the poor under the headings of justice (70–74), overcoming marginalization (77), the moral priorities of the nation (86–92), and the role of government (123), and by implication, throughout this section. Although the section in chapter III titled "Poverty" makes recommendations largely in the area of welfare policy, the topic of the poor comes up throughout the policy questions. Yet again, in chapter IV, which suggests that the "unfinished business of the American experiment" calls for new forms of partnership, the impact of policies on the poor is once more invoked as a criterion for judging them. Thus the letter as a whole is like a musical composition in which similar melodic materials reappear in the various movements under different harmonic and rhythmic guises.

Further on, the bishops state that their positions on policy issues "do not carry the same moral authority as our statements of universal moral principles and formal church teaching" (135). They say they "expect debate" on the policy questions, implying that they expect agreement on their principles, though not clearly stating so. Opponents, however, are not likely to reject generally stated principles, but rather to challenge the selection of which principles are to be made most prominent and which are to be ignored or subordinated.

The principles from Catholic social teaching are not primarily a device to lead into a particular set of policy proposals. Rather, the principles themselves are meant to question certain values and certain largely unconscious ways of looking at things and to offer something of an alternate language. To illustrate the problem, on what basis should I be concerned for Midwest families losing their farms—after all, wasn't it they who borrowed over their heads? As an urbanite a half continent away, I might be tempted to believe that we will be better served if we allow market forces to do their work, even if that means "weeding out" many farm families and rural communities.

To take another example, why should the fact that the numbers of stretch limos and homeless people seem to grow proportionately be of anything more to me than a sociological curiosity? As *Habits of the Heart* points out, we find it hard to justify a more inclusive view; we have no language for expressing it. In this part of *Economic Justice for All* the bishops are drawing on the tradition of Catholic social teaching to supply some elements of such a language.

"Human life is life in community," they assert, immediately noting that the command to love God and neighbor are the heart and soul of morality. The doctrine of the Trinity—Father, Son and Holy Spirit—"shows that being a person means being united to other persons in mutual love." The implication is that relatedness to others is not based, for example, on some kind of contract or a cost-benefit calculus but is grounded in what for Christians is the deepest root of reality.

There follows a discussion of justice, especially that of "basic or minimal justice," understood as providing norms for "the *minimum* levels of mutual care and respect that all persons owe to each other in an imperfect world." Their reflection follows traditional moral theology with its division into commutative justice (for example, as in contracts), distributive justice, and social justice.

As its name implies, distributive justice refers to the "allocation of income, wealth and power in society." Although Catholic social teaching does not insist on "a flat, arithmetical equality of income and wealth," it does "challenge economic arrangements that leave large numbers of people impoverished" (74). The community must help people to meet what is required for a human life, "unless an absolute scarcity of resources makes this strictly impossible. No such scarcity exists in the United States today" (70). The measured language should not blunt the impact: the U.S. Catholic bishops are saying that the extent of poverty currently existing in the United States is unjustifiable.

Justice demands more than meeting physical needs. Social justice *"implies that persons have an obligation to be active and productive participants in the life of society and that society has a duty to enable them to participate in this way"* (71; emphasis in original).

Distributive justice and social justice come together in what the bishops call "basic justice," which both calls for a "floor of material well-being on which all can stand" (74) and "demands the establishment of minimum levels of participation in the life of the human community for all persons." "The ultimate injustice is for a person or group to be treated actively or abandoned passively as if they were nonmembers of the human race" (77).

Such marginalization can take many forms: political restrictions or repression, or the downward cycle of poverty in which the "poor, the disabled, and the unemployed too often are simply left behind" and whole countries are marginalized from the international economic order. "These patterns of exclusion are created by free human beings. In this sense they can be called forms of social sin. Acquiescence in them or failure to correct them when it is possible to do so is a sinful dereliction of Christian duty" (77). Since the notion of "social sin" is generally resisted by theological conservatives, who insist that sin can be attributed only to responsible individuals, its inclusion here is all the more significant.

Next the bishops take up human rights, which they see as grounded in basic justice. Following Catholic social teaching and especially Pope John XXIII's encyclical *Peace on Earth* and the U.N. Universal Declaration of Human Rights, they mention the civil and political rights to freedom of speech, worship, and assembly but also economic rights: "the rights to life, food, clothing, shelter, rest, medical care, and basic education," which are "indispensable to the protection of human dignity." Such rights entail the "right to earn a living" and "a right to security in the event of sickness, unemployment, and old age." Such "fundamental personal rights—civil and political as well as social and economic—state the minimum conditions for social institutions that respect human dignity, social solidarity, and justice. . . . Any denial of these rights harms persons and wounds the human community" (80).

Although this statement is squarely in line with Catholic social teaching, it is rather at odds with prevailing thought patterns in the United States. Conservatives reject the very notion of economic and social *rights*. They do not object to formulating such matters in terms of goals to be attained, but they insist that the language of rights should be restricted to the relatively narrow range of political freedoms associated with Western democracies. Rights are invoked to defend the individual from the encroachments of the state. Liberals may sympathize with the notion of economic and social rights, and perhaps assent to it, but they are hard pressed to justify them from within the larger historical liberal tradition.

Recognizing that the "mode of implementation" of social and economic rights is different from that required for civil and political rights, the bishops nevertheless assert that "both kinds of rights call for positive action to create social and political institutions that enable all persons to become active members of society." Just as the recognition of civil and political rights has been achieved through a "long and vigorous history of creating the institutions of constitutional government," the establishment of the "full range of social and economic rights" will require a similar effort. Such an effort will require "a new cultural consensus that the basic economic conditions of human welfare are essential to human dignity and are due persons by right."

Grounded in these considerations on love, basic justice, and human rights the bishops go on to make observations on "moral priorities for the nation," in a kind of reprise of the themes thus far created. They argue that "As individuals and as a nation . . . we are called to make a fundamental 'option for the poor,' " borrowing the latter phrase from Latin American Catholics. This is "not an adversarial slogan that pits one group or class against another. Rather it states that the deprivation and powerlessness of the poor wounds the whole community" (87–88). The bishops argue that "meeting fundamental human needs must come before the fulfillment of desires for luxury consumer goods, for profits not conducive to the common good and for unnecessary military hardware." Policies should strengthen family life.

WORKERS, BUSINESS PEOPLE, CITIZENS

From norms the bishops move on to major economic actors. The question under the surface seems to be the role of public and private spheres. The bishops may have in mind some of their critics, who accuse them of granting too large a role to the government. Some of the topics dealt with at this point are further developed elsewhere in the letter.

At this point the bishops make explicit reference to Pope John Paul II's 1981 encyclical *Laborem Exercens* (*On Human Work*), citing his statement that "human work is a key, probably the essential key, to the whole social question." Traditional Catholic social teaching tended to be grounded in a consideration of the spiritual qualities of the human being, especially reason and free will. John Paul II's letter represents a new development insofar as it reflects a humanism that embraces *homo faber*, seeing what is distinctively human in the ability to build and transform as well as to reason and contemplate.

The bishops note that the pope's definition of work includes not only agriculture and industry but also activities such as child care, politics, and so forth. Such an inclusive definition, it may be pointed out, coincides neither with Marxism, which distinguishes between "productive" work (transforming nature and producing physically measureable objects) and "nonproductive" work (bureaucracy, management, and so forth), nor with capitalism, which equates work with what is remunerated.

Work, say the bishops, has a "threefold moral significance": through it people exercise "the distinctive human capacity for self-expression and self-realization," satisfy their material needs, and serve the larger community. These somewhat bland observations provide a humanistic basis for some judgments made later.

In taking up the situation of labor properly so called, the bishops reiterate that employment is a right and emphasize workers' rights to wages and benefits, as well as their rights to organize and to go on strike. They pointedly state, "No one may deny the right to organize without attacking human dignity itself. Therefore, we firmly oppose organized efforts, such as those regrettably now seen in this country, to break existing unions and prevent workers from organizing" (104). Implicitly responding to management's cry that high wages are making U.S. industry uncompetitive, the bishops note that wages are only one such factor and that "it is unfair to expect unions to make concessions if managers and shareholders do not make at least equal sacrifices."

This whole section reaffirms the U.S. Catholic church's long-standing association with organized labor, which has its roots in the experience of immigrants, especially the Irish, in large Eastern and Midwestern cities at the turn of the century. However, while fully asserting the rights of labor and praising unions for their accomplishments, the bishops also urge them to do more to elim-inate racial and sexual discrimination and to become more im-aginative and creative in order to face present challenges.

The next section develops the responsibilities of business people more explicitly than has been characteristic of previous Catholic social teaching. "Business people, managers, investors, and fi-nanciers follow a vital Christian vocation when they act respon-sibly and seek the common good" (117). The overall tone is one of respect for this vocation and an acknowledgment of the seri-ousness of the decisions business people are called upon to make. The letter is intended to aid them in such decisions.

However, business people should see themselves as "trustees of the resources at their disposal. No one can ever own capital re-sources absolutely or control their use without regard for others and society as a whole" (112)—especially land and natural re-sources. A broad managerial vision is needed, one that does not simply pursue short-term profits.

"The Catholic tradition has long defended the right to private ownership of productive property," a right said to enlarge "our capacity for creativity and initiative" (114). The bishops no doubt have a great deal of admiration for the virtues entailed in managing small and medium-size businesses. "Widespread distribution of property can help avoid excessive concentration of economic and political power. . . . [O]wnership should be made possible for a broad sector of our population." Only occasionally and inciden-tally, however, do they raise questions about the impact of giant corporations.

One of the most revered and most cited notions in Catholic social teaching has been the "principle of subsidiarity," attributed to Pius XI. As the bishops put it, "in order to protect basic justice, government should undertake only those initiatives that exceed the capacity of individuals or private groups acting independently. Government should not replace or destroy smaller communities and individual initiative" (124). Part of the philosophical basis for this principle is "the traditional distinction between society and the state. . . . Social life is richer than governmental power can encompass." This statement is clearly a rejection of totalitarian or statist approaches. However, the bishops insist that "government has a moral function: protecting human rights and securing basic justice for all members of the commonwealth" (121, 122, 124).

MERELY REFORMIST?

One of the media triggers during the preparation of *Economic Justice for All* was the hint that the bishops might be questioning capitalism and advocating radical changes. As they begin chapter III, "Selected Economic Policy Issues," they pause to deal head-on with the capitalism-socialism question. They first stake out two extreme positions: on one side stand those who "argue that an unfettered free-market economy . . . provides the greatest possible liberty, material welfare and equity" and who thus believe that it is best to intervene as little as possible; on the other side are those who "argue that the capitalist system is inherently inequitable and therefore contradictory to the demands of Christian morality, for it is based on acquisitiveness, competition and self-centered individualism," and hence it "must be replaced by a radically different system that abolishes private property, the profit motive and the free market" (128).

Not surprisingly they are led to reject these extremes, both by Catholic social teaching and by the American experience. The Church "is not bound to any particular economic, political, or social system; it has lived with many forms of economic and social organization and will continue to do so." Noting that "we live in a 'mixed' economic system which is the product of a long history of reform and adjustment," the bishops situate their own effort "in the spirit of this American pragmatic tradition of reform" (130–31).

At the very moment they are acknowledging that their own focus is on reform, however, they emphasize that larger issues cannot be ignored, phrasing them in the form of questions:

> Does our economic system place more emphasis on maximizing profits than on meeting human needs and fostering human dignity? Does our economy distribute its benefits equitably or does it concentrate power and resources in the hands of a few? Does it promote excessive materialism and individualism? Does it adequately protect the environment and the nation's natural resources? Does it direct too many scarce resources to military purposes? (132)

To criticize the letter as anticapitalist is to misread it: it clearly assumes the modern Western welfare state, especially in its observations on policy. However, to the extent that it proposes criteria for a truly human economy, raises questions about present "economic arrangements," and emphasizes the human capacity to shape institutions, the letter's explicit reformist stand may be belied by an implicitly radical logic and by the bishops' urging of "continuing exploration of these systemic questions in a more comprehensive way than this document permits." This is no hidden agenda. There is no ready-made model for replacing the present economy. Any deep-seated transformation of the present capitalist economy would occur only through a historical process of struggle filled with surprises. Systemic questions are secondary in the letter; only occasionally do they take the melodic line.

POLICY QUESTIONS

In chapter III the letter reaches its most specific level as the bishops take up policy questions under the headings of employment, poverty, food and agriculture, and the relationship of the United States to the underdeveloped world. They emphasize that their treatment of these issues "does not constitute a comprehensive analysis of the U.S. economy" but rather that they "exemplify the interaction of moral values and economic issues." They are not presenting a "technical blueprint for economic reform," but seeking to "foster a serious moral analysis leading to a more just economy" (133).

This section represents a genuine innovation in Catholic pastoral letters. Classic papal documents are quite general, and even though national bishops' conferences sometimes make statements on public issues (in Latin America, land reform), pastoral letters remain at a general level. That is true even of the well-known documents from the Latin American bishops assembled in Medellín, Colombia (1968), and Puebla, Mexico (1979), with all their ringing denunciation of injustice and calls for basic changes.

Archbishop Weakland explains that the bishops felt the letter should "show to the American Catholic population how the principles from the biblical and ethical vision affect daily life and the economic decisions of both nation and individuals," since "the American mentality is highly inductive and must begin almost necessarily with the concrete in order to understand what the principles are all about." They recognized the problem that economic factors constantly change and that it is hard to come to concrete options.

Their decision to focus on four areas (employment, poverty, farm crisis, and United States–Third World relations) represents an option from among others and is perhaps less than satisfactory. One can imagine a more comprehensive effort, one that would have attempted, for example, to situate the economy more clearly in an ecological context or would have outlined the major historic phases of the U.S. economy in order better to understand the present. The pastoral letter does not provide a comprehensive framework of interpretation. To have attempted such a framework, however, might have provoked even more charges that the bishops were imposing an ideological viewpoint and polarized the atmosphere even more. The very fact that the policy sections are intended primarily as examples of how to bring moral considerations to bear—the very unfinished nature of the document—serves as an invitation for further development of Catholic social thought.

Although, in brainstorming at early sessions, the drafting committee drew up a list of perhaps forty potential topics, pastoral concern soon narrowed the list to a few. In a status report to other bishops in November 1983, Weakland listed "employment generation. . . . Adequate income for the poor and disadvantaged, ... Trade: U.S. and developing countries . . . and economic planning and policy" as the four issues to be discussed. However, as the U.S. farm crisis grew, a number of midwestern bishops, including Bishop George Speltz, who was on the drafting committee, were urging that agriculture be one of those topics. Because the decision to include it came relatively late, the section on agriculture was not ready when the first public draft of the letter appeared in November 1984. Meanwhile, the question of planning, which Weakland himself realized was of a different nature, was moved to what became chapter IV.

The treatment of each of these issues follows a similar pattern, proceeding from a factual and statistical description to guidelines to policy recommendations.

BATTLING UNEMPLOYMENT

In order to situate the bishops' positions on both unemployment and poverty, it is useful to recall that in mid-1980s America it was fashionable to see the "Great Society" programs as having failed and to trust in market forces to make the United States more competitive by weeding out the inefficient and incompetent. The president could please crowds with anecdotes about welfare cheaters while Nancy Reagan's ten-thousand-dollar dress led to only bemused protest and possibly helped many upward strivers feel comfortable with their own more modest consumerism. The U.S. public was told it could afford fewer services and should take up the slack with volunteerism. The bishops wrote in such a context of ascendant neoconservatism and their critics began to dispute publicly with them even during their deliberations (see next chapter).

Their bedrock assertion is that "Employment is a basic right, a right which protects the freedom of all to participate in the economic life of society" (137). They then note that joblessness is on the rise, with about 8 million people (7 percent of the labor force) looking for a job. When those who have given up looking for work and those who want full-time work but are working part-time are factored in, about one-eighth of the work force is directly affected by unemployment. In contrast to the general experience since 1950, when the unemployment rate hovered at around 3 to 4 percent, except during recessions, it has remained above 7 percent during most of the 1980s. (These figures of course reflect 1986, when the letter was published. During 1987, unemployment inched downward to about 6 percent and continued to decline during 1988.) Both policymakers and the public, say the bishops, have shown a willingness to "tolerate" rates of 6 or 7 percent or even more.

Blacks, Hispanics, Native Americans, young people, and women are disproportionately unemployed. Our society is telling them, "We don't need your talent. We don't need your initiative. We don't need *you*" (141). The bishops note the costs to individuals and families and to society itself. They conclude that current levels of unemployment are "intolerable, and . . . impose . . . a moral obligation to work for policies that will reduce joblessness" (143). Full employment, however, "may require major adjustments and creative strategies that go beyond the limits of existing policies and institutions, but it is a task we must undertake" (150).

They immediately recognize the complexity of the problem: more people, especially women, are joining the labor force; technological changes mean that most new jobs are low-paying. Further factors are competition from overseas labor, discrimination against minorities and women, and high levels of defense spending, which is less labor-intensive than other sectors of the economy.

When the first draft stated that an unemployment rate "in the range of 3 or 4 percent is a reasonable definition of full employment in the United States today," critics asked whence came the episcopal authority to define economic matters so precisely. In the final version they express themselves more circumspectly, while still holding their ground. They note that "the acceptance of present unemployment rates would have been unthinkable twenty years ago. It should be regarded as intolerable today." Acknowledging that there are trade-offs and complexities, they nevertheless believe "that 6 to 7 percent unemployment is neither inevitable nor acceptable."

In keeping with their intent to provide more of a moral impetus than detailed prescriptions, the bishops state, "We must first establish a consensus that everyone has a right to employment." It is assumed that most new jobs will come from the private sector. They recommend a "careful mix of general economic policies and targeted employment programs." They urge that fiscal and monetary policies, such as federal spending and tax and interest rate policies, be coordinated so as to achieve full employment. They are clearly siding with economists who are unconvinced that existing unemployment rates must be accepted in order to control inflation, but they offer nothing more specific.

As targeted programs, the bishops recommend the expansion of "job training and apprenticeship programs in the private sector administered and supported jointly by business, labor unions and government." They also urge "increased support for direct job-creation programs focused on the long-term unemployed and those with special needs." They note that such jobs should be aimed at "meeting society's unmet needs" and give numerous examples: work on parks and recreation facilities, bridges and highways, low-income housing, educational systems, day care, and help for senior citizens. "Surely we have the capacity to match these needs by giving Americans who are anxious to work a chance for productive employment in jobs that are waiting to be done" (162–65).

Most of the foregoing recommendations could be put into effect without major institutional changes. In addition the bishops list a number of alternative approaches, some of which would demand longer-range changes: "job sharing, flex time and a reduced work-week," "limiting or abolishing compulsory overtime work," and discouraging the use of part-time workers who do not receive fringe benefits. They also urge "pay equity between men and women." Finally, they broach the subject of converting some military production to "more peaceful and socially productive purposes" (167–68).

POVERTY AND POLICY

"Dealing with poverty is not a luxury to which our nation can attend when it finds the time and resources. Rather, it is a moral imperative of the highest priority" (170). Again, the letter rebukes the ethos of the 1980s.

By the government's own figures, note the bishops, more than 33 million Americans—one in seven—are poor. Moreover, the poverty rate has increased by a third since 1973. The bishops state that they have seen the "faces of poverty" in homeless people on subway grates, mental patients released from state hospitals, and in thousands standing in line at soup kitchens.

As they did with regard to unemployment, the bishops sketch the characteristics of current poverty, noting how it affects children, women, and minorities. Indeed, this may be the section most directly sensitive to women's concerns, as the document notes the "feminization of poverty." (The expression, used in a footnote, was coined in 1980 by Dr. Diana Pearce. She provided written testimony for one of the bishops' hearings.) Women earn only 61 percent of what men earn and 60 percent of all women work in only ten occupations. Contrary to what one might expect, the bishops show little sign of preference for a "traditional" housewife role but more neutrally note changes in family life, the problems faced by women after marriages break up, the fact that child raising constricts their career choices, and that most divorced or separated women do not get child-support payments. They also note that while the poverty rate for whites is one out of nine, for blacks it is one out of three, and for Hispanics one out of four. Black families earn only 55 percent of white-family income, and the discrepancy is growing.

The bishops then point out "the very uneven distribution of wealth and income" in the United States. The top 2 percent of families (whose annual income is over $125,000) hold 54 percent of all financial wealth. The top one-fifth of the population receives 42.9 percent of income, while the bottom 20 percent receives only 4.7 percent. The United States is "among the more unequal" of industrialized nations in income distribution and the gap has been growing during the last decade. These inequities "reflect the uneven distribution of power in our society." Catholic social teaching "does not require absolute equality," and in fact some degree of inequality "may be considered desirable for economic and social reasons," that is, to provide incentives for risk taking. However, such inequality should be evaluated in terms of the needs of the poor and the level of participation in society. Thus, there is "a strong presumption against extreme inequality of income and wealth as long as there are poor, hungry and homeless people in our midst." Such inequalities undermine "social solidarity and community." Having carefully outlined all these arguments, the bishops come to one of their more controversial judgments: "we find the disparities of income and wealth in the United States to be unacceptable" (183–85). Critics see this judgment as another example of bishops overstepping the bounds of their authority and competence.

As in the case of unemployment, their prescription is first in the realm of ethos. The "principle of social solidarity" suggests that "fundamental changes in social and economic structures" may be required. Solutions, moreover, should "enable people to take control of their own lives."

The letter takes issue with those who see past and existing programs as failures (most notably, Charles Murray, *Losing Ground*, cited in a footnote). "During the 1960s and early 1970s the official poverty rate was cut in half. . . . It is estimated . . .

that in the late 1970s federal benefit programs were lifting out of poverty about 70 percent of those who would have otherwise been poor." The success of Social Security, Medicare, and Medicaid should make us confident that we can design effective programs.

There are strong words about stereotypes: that most of the poor are black, that people stay on welfare for a long time and that most of them could work. With statistics the bishops refute each of these stereotypes and then "ask everyone to refrain from actions, words or attitudes that stigmatize the poor, that exaggerate the benefits received by the poor, and that inflate the amount of fraud in welfare payments." Generous subsidies for individuals and corporations are "taken for granted and not even called benefits but entitlements," whereas "programs for the poor are called handouts and receive a great deal of critical attention, even though they account for less than 10 percent of the federal budget" (193–94).

Their recommendations emphasize employment opportunity, raising the minimum wage to keep pace with inflation, eliminating employment discrimination, self-help programs for the poor, tax reform, and increased educational opportunity. They devote specific attention to the question of family stability. "The high rate of divorce and the alarming extent of teen-age pregnancies . . . are distressing signs of the breakdown of traditional family values." These trends are said to be present in all sectors of society but are more damaging among the poor (195–209).

The most specific recommendations concern welfare reform. Programs should be redesigned to help people become self-sufficient through employment. People should receive adequate support: "At present only 4 percent of poor families with children receive enough cash welfare benefits to lift them out of poverty" (212). Citing the disparity in monthly AFDC payments between Mississippi ($96) and Vermont ($558), the bishops urge the establishment and funding of "national minimum-benefit levels and eligibility standards." Such payments should be adjusted for inflation just as they are for the aged, the disabled, and veterans. The practice of limiting AFDC to single-parent (usually women) families should be extended to two-parent families "so that fathers who are unemployed or poorly paid do not have to leave home in order for their children to receive help."

As they did when dealing with unemployment, the bishops end this section by mentioning proposals of a longer-range nature, such as a family allowance or children's allowance and a "negative income tax" (with credit given to Milton Friedman).

LAND, FOOD, AND FARM FAMILIES

The third major policy section focuses on two areas of concern: the farm bankruptcies and foreclosures that are leading to the loss of a whole way of life for some people and increased land concentration by corporations, and the ecological destruction caused by current agricultural practices.

A transition passage notes that the test of an economy "is its ability to meet the essential human needs of this generation and future generations in an equitable fashion." In this allusion to ecological dimensions, the bishops admit that Catholic social teaching in this regard "is still in the process of development" (281). Along with one paragraph in the introduction (12), it is only in the passages dealing with agriculture that the letter shows significant ecological consciousness.

Historically, say the bishops, U.S. agricultural policy has striven both to assure a wide distribution of land to owner-operators and to keep food costs low for consumers. However, from a high of 7 million farms in the 1930s the number declined to 2.4 million in 1983. Only 3 percent of the population is now engaged in producing food. Nearly half of all food production comes from the 4 percent of farms with over $200,000 in gross sales, which are often run not by families but by hired managers. At the opposite extreme, nearly three-quarters of farms are small and today often run by part-time farmers. The bishops are most concerned about the remaining 24 percent of farms (grossing between $40,000 and $200,000), the family farms whose existence is presently threatened. They point to four areas of concern: increasing land concentration; the loss of diversity and richness in American society through the decay of rural communities; environmental degradation due to soil erosion, water depletion, pollution, and so forth; and the situation of blacks and Hispanics in agriculture.

Turning to guidelines, they urge that "moderate-sized farms operated by families on a full-time basis" should be preserved and protected. This position follows from their support for a wide distribution of productive property. Furthermore, the interests of consumers are better protected when farms are operated by families who are likely to persevere through hard times as opposed to the behavior of "nonfarm corporations that enter agriculture in search of high profits" and may cut back or even close operations "without regard to the impact on the community or on the food system" (234). Because it is a valuable way of life, farming should be protected.

Policy recommendations spell out the implications more specifically. The bishops call for "special measures to assist otherwise viable family farms that are threatened with bankruptcy or foreclosure . . . emergency credit, reduced rates of interest, and programs of debt restructuring." Lending institutions should be aided. Somewhat more controversially, the letter urges a reassessment of federal farm programs, "whose benefits now go disproportionately to the largest farmers." Both income-support programs and price-support payments should be limited and reoriented so as to serve moderate and small farmers. Tax laws, which currently encourage use of agriculture by nonfarmers for tax shelters should be reassessed. Even more provocatively, the bishops support "a progressive land tax on farm acreage to discourage the accumulation of excessively large holdings." As if to answer criticism of such tampering with market mechanisms, they immediately point to studies indicating that "medium-sized commercial farms achieve most of the technical cost efficiencies" available today. Their only recommendation with regard to the environment is that the public set standards and bear a share of the cost. Finally they urge solidarity in the farm community so as to overcome individualism; specifically, they believe farmers should not oppose unionization efforts by farmworkers (242–250).

THE UNITED STATES AND THE DEVELOPING NATIONS

In choosing to deal with unemployment, poverty, and the farm crisis, the bishops were motivated by their own pastoral experience. Although the situation of the Third World is more remote, something comparable was at work. Bishop William Weigand of Salt Lake City, who was on the drafting committee, had worked as a priest for a number of years in Latin America. In addition, the bishops consulted with Third World economists and social scientists (September 12–13, 1985) and with a group of Latin American bishops and two members of the Vatican's Pontifical Justice and Peace Commission (April 16–17, 1986). Since the 1960s Catholic social teaching has considered questions of development and the impact of the international economic order on poor countries.

Opening this section, the bishops point to the "fact of interdependence," but go on to note that developing countries "often perceive themselves more as *dependent* on the industrialized countries, especially the United States." This is a clear allusion to the "dependency theories," that arose in Latin America in the 1950s and 1960s. Rejecting the conventional assumption that Third World poverty is due to "backwardness," dependency theorists examined the structures of the international economy controlled by developed capitalist countries. By speaking of "perception," the bishops give voice to a dependency perspective without committing themselves to it. "Subordinated" to the wealthy countries by trade patterns, borrowing terms, behavior of investors, and so forth, and subject to cultural penetration, developing countries are said to be "junior partners at best" (253).

After noting that 800 million of the world's people live in absolute poverty and nearly half a billion are chronically hungry, the bishops state that "their misery is not the inevitable result of the march of history or of the intrinsic nature of particular cultures, but of human decisions and human institutions" (254).

They then point to "three sets of actors" (nations, multilateral agencies, and transnational corporations and banks) and state that "the moral task is to devise rules for the major actors that will move them toward a just international order." An especially "vexing" problem is that of "reconciling the transnational corporations' profit orientation with the common good that they . . . are supposed to serve" (255–56).

In seeking principles to apply, the bishops transpose some of their basic themes (Christian love, universal justice, human rights, the special place of the poor) into an international key. For example, they note that basic justice implies that people are entitled to "participate in the increasingly interdependent global economy in a way that ensures their freedom and dignity. . . . We want a world that works fairly for all." Since standard foreign-policy analysis deals with calculations of power and definitions of interest, and the poor are, "by definition, not powerful," "we have to go beyond economic gain or national security as a starting point for the policy dialogue. We want to stand with the poor everywhere" (258–60).

In preparing the ground for what they have to say about policy, the bishops reiterate their conviction that there is a need for a "political entity . . . with the responsibility and power to promote the global common good." They also lament the tendency of the United States to base its assistance to the Third World "on an East-West assessment of North-South problems, at the expense of basic human needs and economic development." A footnote refers to the November 1983 interagency report prepared under Frank Carlucci (subsequently destined to replace Admiral John Poindexter at the National Security Council and Caspar Weinberger at the Pentagon) that recommended that U.S. military and economic aid be coordinated and that U.S. security concerns be a primary criterion for all aid. They note that in North-South negotiations the United States has often come to be cast "in the role of resisting developing-country proposals without advancing realistic ones of our own." The bishops call on the United States to take up a policy that would "reflect our traditional regard for human rights and our concern for social progress" (261–64). As will be noted in the next chapter, it is just such an unquestioning assumption of the essentially benign nature of U.S. presence in the Third World that more radical critics find exasperating.

Proposed policy guidelines are organized around aid, trade, finance, investment, and the world food problem. Noting that the United States stands "almost last" among the seventeen industrialized nations in the percentage of its GNP devoted to foreign aid, the bishops urge a "more affirmative role," especially in multilateral institutions. On trade they simply raise some ethical questions.

Perhaps their most specific and pointed observations appear in the section on finance, which is in fact largely devoted to the debt crisis. They eschew simplistic explanations (e.g., that the countries themselves must shoulder all the blame). Echoing Third World countries, they state that "the global *system* of finance, development, and trade established by the Bretton Woods Conference in 1944—the World Bank, the International Monetary Fund (IMF), and the GATT . . . seems incapable, without basic changes, of helping the debtor countries—which had no part in its creation—manage their increasingly untenable debt situation effectively and equitably" (273). They issue a reminder that the crisis "affects people." "It is the poorest people who suffer most from the austerity measures" required by the IMF, just as they "suffer most when commodity prices fall, when food cannot be imported or they cannot buy it, and when natural disasters occur." Given their preferential option for the poor, the bishops say, they cannot remain silent.

A number of ways of dealing with the debt crisis are suggested:

> moratorium on payments, conversion of some dollar-denominated debt into local-currency debt, creditors' accepting a share of the burden by partially writing-down selected loans, capitalizing interest, or perhaps outright cancellation. (274)

The message is: all possibilities should be explored. The bishops distinguish between the poorest countries (e.g., in sub-Saharan Africa), for whom cancellation of debts to governments would be especially appropriate, and the better-off debtor countries (e.g., in Latin America), which should be enabled "to adjust their debts without penalizing the poor" (276).

The letter acknowledges the positive role that can be played by private investment in developing countries. Care must be taken to avoid perpetuating dependency, augmenting inequalities, exploiting workers, or serving elites at the cost of the majority. The most specific recommendation is the development of "a code of conduct for foreign corporations that recognizes their quasi-public character" (280).

A final topic, the world food problem, oscillates between the need to bring about long-term solutions through development of food production, especially among small farmers, and the short-term obligation to provide sufficient food aid to meet emergencies. "Relief and prevention of their hunger cannot be "left to the arithmetic of the marketplace" (282). Here they acknowledge the role of population growth and state that "the Church fully supports the need for all to exercise responsible parenthood." Population policies "must be designed as part of an overall strategy of integral human development," avoiding coercion. Given the Church's official stand against "artificial" contraception, this section may be regarded as restrained.

Once more the bishops point to the disproportion between the monies spent on the arms race and those spent on development. *"Rather than promoting U.S. arms sales, especially to countries that cannot afford them, we should be campaigning for an international agreement to reduce this lethal trade"* (289; emphasis in original).

The crisis in the international economic order offers the United States the opportunity "to launch a worldwide campaign for justice and economic rights to match the still incomplete, but encouraging, political democracy we have achieved in the United States with so much pain and sacrifice." To restructure the international order "will require sacrifices of at least the scope of those we have made over the years in building our own nation." Leadership and vision are needed. In closing this section the bishops state, *"we call for a U.S. international economic policy designed to empower*

*people everywhere and enable them to continue to develop a sense
of their own worth, improve the quality of their lives and ensure
that the benefits of economic growth are shared equitably* (292,
emphasis in original).

Facing the obvious objection that what they propose in these
four policy areas would be expensive, the bishops once more
mention the $300 billion spent for military purposes and con-
clude, "In the end, the question is not whether the United States
can provide the necessary funds to meet our social needs, but
whether we have the political will to do so" (294).

A NEW AMERICAN EXPERIMENT

Like the peace pastoral, which moved from a critique of present
policies to more far-reaching, even visionary proposals, *Economic
Justice for All* offers, in chapter IV, longer-range perspectives on
the U.S. economy. The basic argument is that there is "unfinished
business" in the "American experiment."

> The nation's founders took daring steps to create structures
> of participation, mutual accountability, and widely distrib-
> uted power to ensure the political rights and freedoms of all.
> We believe that similar steps are needed today to expand
> economic participation, broaden the sharing of economic
> power, and make economic decisions more accountable to
> the common good. (297; see also 95 and "Message," 21)

This sounds like a call for "economic democracy," a concept used
by some who appeared at the bishops' hearings (Gar Alperovitz)
or are cited in the footnotes (Martin Carnoy, Derek Shearer,
Robert Dahl). Although the term itself was used in the first draft,
the closest the letter itself comes to the term is the expression "a
new experiment in bringing democratic ideals to economic life"
(298).

In the bishops' view, "a greater spirit of partnership and team-
work is needed; competition alone will not do the job." They

organize their reflections starting at the level of firms and move up to the regional, national, and international levels.

At the firm level the problem is that although many different people and groups (workers, managers, shareholders, surrounding community, and so forth) contribute to the enterprise and have a stake in it, "present structures of accountability . . . do not acknowledge all these contributions or protect these stakes." Hence, "new institutional mechanisms for accountability" are needed (298). Possibilities include employee profit sharing or acquiring stock, giving employees a greater voice in determining work conditions, cooperative ownership, and extending shareholding to a far larger number of Americans (300). The general thrust of these recommendations is buttressed with references to Catholic social teaching.

These recommendations are made in general terms. Again the bishops endorse the rights of labor and labor unions. When decisions over whether to close plants or transfer capital arise, it is "patently unjust to deny workers any role in shaping the outcome of these difficult choices" (303). Indeed, one senses that when they were writing this chapter the bishops had in mind the devastating impact of such closures and transfers in their own dioceses. While such decisions may sometimes be necessary, "a collaborative and mutually accountable model of industrial organization" would not have workers carry all the burdens of transition. Since the firm's capital is partly due to their labor, workers "have a right to be informed in advance when such decisions are under consideration, a right to negotiate with management about possible alternatives, and a right to fair compensation and assistance with retraining and relocation expenses should these be necessary" (303).

The letter raises the question of the role of shareholders. The bishops note that "Corporate merger and hostile takeovers may bring greater benefits to shareholders, but they often lead to decreased concern for the well-being of local communities and make towns and cities more vulnerable to decisions made from afar." However, the "governing criterion" for relationship between shareholders and management is "return on investment." The bishops do not believe that "this is an adequate rationale for shareholder decisions," but their only proposal is for "long-term research and experimentation in this area" (305–306).

The next section, on local and regional cooperation, views the same situation from the side of the community. The bishops recognize the "vicious cycle" in areas of high unemployment, with their "[l]ack of financial resources, limited entrepreneurial skill, blighted and unsafe environments, and a deteriorating infrastructure." Their response is essentially an exhortation for a "communitywide cooperative strategy," in which churches should play a prominent role.

A PLEA FOR PLANNING

In the next section, "Partnership in the Development of National Policies," the letter weighs in on the side of some form of economic planning. The bishops note that "the mere mention of economic planning is likely to produce a strong negative reaction in U.S. society. It conjures up images of centralized planning boards, command economies, inefficient bureaucracies, and mountains of government paperwork" (316).

Their counterargument is essentially one of fact: many kinds of economic planning are already taking place: by individuals, families, management and labor, towns, cities and regions, state legislatures, and the U.S. Congress. Catholic social teaching does not propose "a single model for political and economic life" for relating these various levels, but there must be a "reasonable coordination among the different parts of the body politic" (317).

On the level of principle they state that "while economic freedom and personal initiative are deservedly esteemed in our society, we have increasingly come to recognize the inescapably social and political nature of the economy. The market is always embedded in a specific social and political context" (313). They go on to mention taxation, monetary policies, defense programs, regulation, and so forth and, further on, note that "a modern economy without governmental interventions of the sort we have alluded to is inconceivable" (318).

As they see it, the task is "to move beyond abstract disputes about whether more or less government intervention is needed, to consideration of creative ways of enabling government and private groups to work together effectively" (314). They suggest three criteria for planning. First, "all parts of society" must cooperate in forming national economic policies. This will require greater cooperation among all citizens and a sharpened concern for the common good. Second, the primary criterion for judging national economic policies should be their impact on the poor and the vulnerable, "those who fall through the cracks of our economy." Third, they once again bring up the "serious distortions" of priorities produced by massive defense spending. The intertwining of the government and the economy is clear in the case of defense industries, which "often depart from the competitive model of free-market capitalism." Devoting so much of the national budget to military purposes has been disastrous to the poor and vulnerable in the United States and elsewhere (318–20).

The bishops' reflections on international cooperation seem to be largely a restatement of themes discussed in the treatment of the United States and the Third World in chapter III. Thus the "unfinished business of the American experiment includes the formation of new international partnerships, especially with the developing countries, based on mutual respect, cooperation, and a dedication to fundamental justice" (322).

PRACTICING WHAT IS PREACHED

In its last chapter, *Economic Justice for All*, like the peace pastoral, seeks to draw conclusions for Catholic spirituality. More provocatively, it asserts that the Church should practice internally the justice it recommends for society at large. Since the present book is concerned with the policy implications of the letters, it would be possible to disregard this question. However, to ignore such

questions entirely would be to miss something essential of the
spirit of the letter. From the letter itself, and from his own writings
and speeches, it is clear that Archbishop Weakland, who is a
Benedictine monk, sees them as an integral part of the letter.

A basic category is that of vocation or calling. Christians are
called to a conversion, a "process that goes on through our entire
life." The bishops point to the connection between worship and
work:

> The body of Christ which worshipers receive in Communion
> is also a reminder of the reconciling power of his death on
> the Cross. It empowers them to work to heal the brokenness
> of society and human relationships and to grow in a spirit
> of self-giving for others. (330)
>
> Together in the community of worship, we are encouraged
> to use the goods of this earth for the benefit of all. In worship
> and in deeds for justice, the Church becomes a "sacrament,"
> a visible sign of that unity in justice and peace that God wills
> for the whole of humanity. (331)

A generation ago, theologians and Vatican II retrieved and rein-
terpreted the idea of "sacrament"—then understood as referring
to the "seven sacraments," baptism, eucharist, and so forth—
applying it to the Church itself. As a "primordial sacrament," the
Church is a living symbol of God's presence in the world. Here
this notion is being taken one step further, in the sense that in
carrying out "deeds for justice," Christians embody such a sign.
To make it more concrete, Christians at a demonstration (a "deed
for justice") may be making the Church a sign of God's presence
in the world.

A section on the "call to holiness" raises questions that should
be taken into account in making personal and family decisions:
"Are we becoming ever more wasteful in a 'throw-away' society?
Are we able to distinguish between our true needs and those thrust
on us by advertising and a society that values consumption more
than saving?" Readers are encouraged to question whether they
are not called to adopt a "simpler lifestyle" (334).

Serious questions are raised about the balance between work and leisure. For some people, work is so tedious or boring that they find fulfillment only off the job; others become "workaholics." Work should be on a human scale. "Why is it one hears so little today about shortening the work week, especially if both parents are working?" (337). Throughout this section, an underlying, though not quite stated, question is what relevance the gospel ideal of poverty has for middle-class America. Unlike some Church people, including Pope John Paul II, the bishops do not criticize "hedonism," but ask probing questions. Further considerations are organized around the traditional concerns of education and family.

As an "economic actor"

> the Church employs many people; it has investments; it has extensive properties for worship and mission. *All the moral principles that govern the just operation of any economic endeavor apply to the Church and its agencies and institutions; indeed the Church should be exemplary.* (347; emphasis in original)

Noting the need for the Church to examine its own role, the bishops go on to make several observations on its own practice. First, they commit themselves and Church institutions to pay adequate salaries, adding immediately that this will require increased contributions. Their statement that "All church institutions must . . . fully recognize the rights of employees to organize and bargain collectively with the institution through whatever association or organization they freely choose" (353) takes on added relevance in the light of the frequent resistance of Catholic institutions, such as hospitals, to unionization. They recognize "the need to be alert particularly to the continuing discrimination against women throughout Church and society," especially in pay scales. Church institutions should examine their investments and make use of their stockholders' voting power to help shape corporate policies or pursue "alternative investment policies." Similarly, the Church should consider alternative uses for buildings that may be underused. Church sponsorship of grass-roots efforts for change are encouraged; the Church's own Campaign for Human Development is praised (see chapter 6).

Besides being an economic actor the Church is a "significant cultural actor." Hence the bishops commit the Church to become a "model of collaboration and participation" for society at large.

As they move to conclude, the bishops state that the letter is "but the beginning of a long process of education, discussion, and action; its contents must be brought to all members of the Church and of society." At one point they present a very long list of topics for further research, including questions scarcely mentioned in the text, such as robotics and automation, "legitimate profit versus greed," migration and its effects, and so forth.

As though to summarize the foregoing many-sided discussion, the letter says we can "ask ourselves one single question: How does our economic system affect the lives of people—all people?

> Since we profess to be members of a "catholic" or universal Church, we all must raise our sights to a concern for the well-being of everyone in the world. Third World debt becomes our problem. Famine and starvation in sub-Saharan Africa become our concern. Rising military expenditures everywhere in the world become part of our fears for the future of this planet. We cannot be content if we see ecological neglect or the squandering of natural resources. (363)

We should see our present economic interdependence as a "moment of grace . . . that can unite all of us in a common community of the human family." We have to move from "our devotion to independence" to interdependence to human solidarity (365).

· 5 ·

MINDING WHOSE BUSINESS?

In order to avoid any accusation of playing politics, the bishops released the first draft of the letter on the economy shortly after the November 1984 election. As already noted, conservative critics leaped to the attack. William Buckley complained of "lumpen clichés." "I hope the bishops recognize," commented White House communications director Patrick Buchanan, "that the greatest enemy of material poverty in human history has been the free enterprise system of the United States." Syndicated columnist David Broder suggested that the right's reaction reflected "conservatism's unease at the shaky moral foundations of its own economics." *USA Today* editorialized that the pastoral "pricks the conscience of the nation—and challenges the myth that the improving economy has helped us all."

Despite the bishops' efforts to avoid using the letter for partisan politics, it was inevitably evaluated differently by critics at different points on the conservative-liberal spectrum.

The most vigorous public discussion took place around the first two public drafts of the letter (November 1984 and October 1985). Commentators hoped to shape the debate and influence the final version. The process also prompted numerous conferences and articles.

In turning to the critics, it is perhaps well to be reminded that it was not the bishops' intention to resolve long-standing economic debates but to bring a moral perspective to bear on fundamental issues in the U.S. economy. Their own letter and the debate over it, however, demonstrate how serious discussion of the ethical dimension involves one's view of the factual elements and the framework used to interpret them.

Predictably, there were those on both right and left who criticized the overall thrust of the letter, while others were largely in agreement but criticized what they saw as shortcomings or suggested further developments. Critiques were more diffuse than those around *The Challenge of Peace,* possibly because the question of nuclear weapons is more sharply focused and positions are more neatly arranged on a continuum from pacifists through "nuclear pacifists" through "realists" to those for whom no amount of deterrence is enough. The hydra-headed nature of economic issues leads to greater diversity.

NOVAK AGAIN

The most systematic response from the right was produced by the Lay Commission on Catholic Social Teaching and the U.S. Economy. The committee of some thirty people itself arose out of an initiative by William E. Simon, former secretary of the treasury, beginning in January 1984. Most committee members were Catholics prominent in public life or the business world, such as J. Peter Grace, Alexander Haig, Walter Hickel, Clare Boothe Luce, all of whom can be reasonably called conservative. One assumes that Michael Novak's previous experience in preparing an alternative to the peace pastoral served as a model for the new endeavor and made Novak a natural choice to serve as

Simon's cochairman. Novak, it should be noted, belongs in the neoconservative camp: he is close to the American Enterprise Institute, for which he has worked, rather than to the Heritage Foundation; his approach to liberals is not a William Buckley-type of amused contempt but an earnest appeal for them to experience an illumination similar to his own. The committee's efforts are part of an ideological offensive in the churches as manifested in the Institute for Religion and Democracy, founded in 1979, and the neoconservative religious publications *This World* and *Catholicism and Crisis* (later shortened to *Crisis*). The proponents of these movements feel that they are doing battle with a left-liberal establishment that has a quasi-monopolistic hold over Church institutions and at the same time that they themselves represent the wave of the future. On the other hand, the fact that for over a decade existing economic structures have required vigorous apologists is itself an indication that their legitimacy is at least in question.

Procedurally, the Lay Commission mirrored the bishops, though on a smaller scale. It held hearings to examine testimony from a number of experts, with a conservative tilt although not exclusively (e.g., Michael Harrington and Diana Pearce appeared). In November 1984 the commission published *Toward the Future: Catholic Social Thought and the U.S. Economy—A Lay Letter* shortly before the public release of the first draft of the pastoral letter on the economy. Novak and the Lay Commission generally became the "contrary view" in standard journalistic procedure.

Although the 1984 document—really a small book—represents a more systematic presentation of the lay commission's views, we will here concentrate on their statement "Liberty and Justice for All" of November 1986, since it is a critique of the third and final draft of the letter the bishops approved later that same month.

At the outset Novak and Simon "commend our bishops for the improvements introduced since their first draft" and say they are "gratified to see how many of the points we raised—particularly concerning the family—have found their way into the bishops' final draft." What Novak and Simon find to praise is primarily the bishops' intentions to lift the poor out of poverty (immediately warning, however, that "economic policies are judged by their results"), the fact that the final draft contains emphatic statements in favor of a capitalist economy, and the fact that the bishops' letter opens up a dialogue.

Despite a number of positive observations about the letter, Novak and Simon go on to list a series of "defects":

> a failure to grasp what makes poor nations into developed nations; deficient understandings of *political economy* (the relative roles of government and the free economy); excessive trust in the state and its officials; an inadequate grasp of crucial concepts such as enterprise, markets, and profits; significant confusions about economic rights; fateful confusions between defense spending and spending on weapons; a preference for "solidarity" over pluralism; and an inadequate exposition of "liberty."

Moreover the bishops are said to use data one-sidedly and to fail to grasp "the distinctive nature of the American experiment in political economy." Since the rest of the statement elaborates on that catalog of defects, the opening acknowledgments are faint praise indeed.

Much of the Lay Commission's 1984 and 1986 statements are variations on themes Novak has been expressing in recent years in works such as *The Spirit of Democratic Capitalism* and *Freedom with Justice*. It is perhaps not unfair to say that he sees it as his intellectual vocation to bring the Catholic church in the United States and elsewhere to recognize the relevance of the American experience—economic as well as political—for Catholic social teaching. While he has a basic respect for Catholic social teaching, he feels it has much to learn. It is from that perspective that he criticizes recent Latin American theology in *Will It Liberate?*

In Novak's eyes the bishops fail in two important respects: they do not understand the causes of poverty and wealth, and they do not understand or sufficiently appreciate the distinctive nature of the American experiment and what it has to teach the rest of the world. In *Toward the Future* Novak is not arguing directly with the bishops at all, but rather with left intellectuals and those within the Church who are persuaded by their analysis. The logic would seem to be that the bishops are partially influenced by their ideas, especially through their staff and the experts with whom they consult.

"We reject as empirically unfounded the proposition that the wealth of some *causes* the poverty of others. We reject as false the proposition that the poverty of poor nations is caused by the wealth of richer nations," say Novak and Simon in *Toward the Future* (50). Although the bishops did not make such a claim, they do show some awareness of the "dependency" type of economic theory elaborated by Third World economists beginning in the 1960s.

In a sense poverty does not need explanation, says Novak, since it has been the normal human condition throughout history. "What is distinctive about our era is the insight that wealth can be created in a sustained way." Among the chief causes of wealth "is culture—meaning, in part the national distribution of human capital, including habits, skills, attitudes and ambitions." Secondly, it has become clear that "institutions of political economy" are important, since some liberate human creativity more than others. "Who can compare South Korea with North Korea, West Germany with East, Kenya with Ethiopia, Hong Kong with mainland China, Taiwan with Vietnam, Japan with Brazil, Australia with Argentina, and not see the difference in economic creativity the institutions of political economy can make?"

"Liberty and Justice for All," the title of Novak's critique is consciously chosen to contrast with the bishops' "Economic Justice for All." " 'Liberty'—in its distinctive American meaning of 'liberty under law' and 'under God'—is the distinctive American gift to the social teaching of the Church." According to Novak, this idea is gaining ground "in both the socialist and the traditionalist world" as nations move toward democracy, freedom of conscience, inquiry, speech, openness, and free economic activism, property rights, markets, incentives, and invention." It is symptomatic that the bishops use the language of "solidarity" rather than that of "pluralism," and their vision seems to be one "not of justice based on liberty, but of an equality of income and wealth." Moreover, the bishops—"unaccountably"—"hardly ever" quote from American presidents, Church leaders, or intellectuals, but rather take their intellectual inspiration from the European or Latin American experience.

In contrast to the bishops who urge a "new American experiment" as bold in the economic realm as the experiment in political democracy launched by the founders, Novak in effect says that the bishops "fail to give full weight to the economic originality of the U.S. experiment." Novak and Simon admit that "there are particular evils, weaknesses, and flaws in our economic structures," but spend no time enumerating them. Their arguing strategy is to relativize the bishops' critique by presenting contrary data. Since they offer no proposals of their own for poverty, unemployment, or the farm crisis, one is left to conclude that they do not envision the need for major institutional changes. Indeed, in a passage toward the end of a short statement accompanying their November 1986 critique, they say that "more important" than any flaws in current economic structures is the "larger breakdown in the moral/cultural traditions upon which our political and economic systems ultimately rest."

> Such critical moral habits as personal responsibility, trust, high aspiration and hard work, marital commitment and strong family life, postponed gratification, and the sustained pursuit of education are at the opposite pole from lax sexual standards, teen-age pregnancy, abortion, single-parent households, and dropping out from school. The moral traditions of the United States, both individual and social, need invigoration. It is in this area, more than in matters of economic expertise, that the bishops have a special role.

That passage perhaps expresses much of the let-them-mind-their-own-business feeling that generated the Novak/Simon critiques, even though it contradicts other passages in which the bishops' contribution to public debate is welcomed. While Novak and Simon expressly distance themselves from those who say the bishops have no right to speak about economic matters, they believe the bishops have "gone beyond the bounds of their authority" both by recommending policies best left to lay authorities and to the democratic process and by lending their authority to policies whose failure could bring their own authority into disrepute.

In fact, examination of the bishops' letter shows concern for family breakdown, divorce, abandonment of children, pregnancies out of wedlock, which "all contribute to the amount of poverty among us." However, the bishops say such phenomena are not limited to the poor but that "one could argue that many of these breakdowns come from the false values found among the more affluent—values which ultimately pervade the whole of society" and urge further study of the connections between affluence and marital breakdowns (343–44).

Significantly Novak and Simon claim to "highly admire" the bishops' summary "Pastoral Message" and object primarily to the specific detail in the letter itself. However, Novak also notes that the letter itself contains "many hidden and partisan 'middle axioms,' ideas that mediate between general principles and matters of fact." When they say that the bishops' document is "unmistakably ideological . . . far more so, apparently, than the bishops intended to be," Novak and Simon imply that the bishops are unwittingly advancing the agenda of ideologues on their staff.

The Novak critique finds the bishops using data one-sidedly. Thus if the bishops' measure of poverty were applied elsewhere, including Western Europe, far more people would be considered poor than in the United States. Moreover, the noncash benefits (e.g., food stamps) given to the poor should be taken into account. In finding distribution of wealth and income in the United States unacceptable, because it does not match that of smaller, more homogeneous nations, such as Sweden, the bishops ignore the fact that in practice the income of families fluctuates. With regard to unemployment, Novak points out that each year 9 percent of Americans voluntarily quit in search of better jobs and that the percentage of civilian Americans over sixteen employed is at a record high (61 percent in 1986 as opposed to 56 percent in 1975).

Given their ideological assumptions and their reading of the signs of the times, it is no wonder that the bishops come up with poor recommendations. In a clever turn of phrase, the bishops are accused of making a "preferential option for the state." While the letter is "by no means a socialist document," it repeatedly gravitates toward "political activism" rather than "economic activism." "Economic development begins from the bottom up, through empowering the poor, not from the top down through extending political privileges."

The bishops' letter offers little to the Third World, since in speaking of foreign aid it ignores the way it is mishandled by elites. Rather than attacking "unfettered markets" and profits, the bishops should pay more attention to what enterprise is all about. Indeed " 'profit' is another word for development." The profit motive is a social discipline, channeling resources into their most creative uses—referring to the bishops' statement about the "vexing" problem of reconciling the profits of transnationals with the common good. For Novak, the problem is not taming an "unfettered market" but getting access to the market for the poor both in the United States and in the Third World, where elites are said to keep markets closed and thwart the enterprise of the poor.

To my knowledge neither the bishops nor any of those closely involved in preparing the letter have responded to Novak and Simon. The bishops had ample opportunity to hear from Novak: he was one of the four participants at the first hearing (November 15, 1981), at which overall approaches to the letter were discussed, and he was the only witness to appear at three hearings.

My main object here has been to present the major objections raised by Novak and Simon. Obviously, a thorough response would require a book. Readers can judge for themselves how cogent the arguments are; I will limit myself to some general observations.*

First, Novak is engaged primarily in polemics, not a humble search for truth. Polemics can of course force one to think, sometimes more than a more objective presentation might. Nevertheless, what stands out most in Novak's treatment is his arguing strategy. Take, for example, the insistence on proper lay and hierarchical/clergy roles. By training, Novak is a philosopher and theologian; in political economy he is an autodidact and hence as "lay" as the bishops (or more so: Bishop Speltz, of the drafting committee, has a degree in economics.) Moreover, through pastoral experience the bishops are no doubt closer to the realities of poverty in the United States than the Lay Commission, which is dominated by CEOs and conservative academics.

The point here is not the relative expertise involved in the two enterprises but the polemical nature of invoking the lay/hierarchy distinction with the implication that specifics in economic matters should be left to endeavors like that of the Lay Committee. Economists themselves are split in their assessments of the letter, liberals generally welcoming it, (neo)conservatives disagreeing (and often questioning the bishops' competence), and radicals praising it for questions asked while finding its interpretive framework inadequate. The *New York Times* economics reporter and columnist Leonard Silk wrote that many economists would agree "that the bishops have brought together competent economic analysis and a clear-eyed view of actual conditions in the United States and other countries." James O'Leary, former vice-chairman of the board of United Trust Company, who has served on eight or ten corporate boards and has a Ph.D. in economics, said the bishops were "right on target." He also said he thought their critique "is widely accepted by the academic economics profession" and that he had shown a copy to the highly respected economist Walter Heller before his death and he had been "ecstatic" over it.

* See my *Liberation Theology* (pp. 180–84) for further comments on Novak's major positions on the economy.

Although the 1986 critique is based to some extent on the bishops' texts, Novak/Simon's major polemic energy goes into defending something the bishops do not attack—American capitalism and indeed capitalism as a system. Thus their most detailed discussion is devoted to explanations for world poverty. As we noted, the bishops discuss that only as the fourth and last topic of chapter III. Although they make a reference to dependency theory and show some sensitivity to Third World perceptions, their attitude toward the causes of poverty is essentially agnostic. Their most important policy concern is that of the Third World debt, about which Novak/Simon say virtually nothing (although in a clever verbal touch they call it a "loan crisis").

Novak seems to feel that he is a lonely crusader doing battle with conventional—and misguided—leftist wisdom, which is rampant among Catholic peace and justice advocates and even reaches into the Church bureaucracy and thus to the hierarchy. His attitude is inaccurate in several ways. First, it should be noted that although structural views of underdevelopment, like dependency theory, have gained respectability since the 1960s, the dominant view—in governments, international agencies, and economics departments—has remained close to what Novak proclaims. If Church people are sympathetic to Third World critiques, it is due to the fact that missionary and development work has given the Church sustained village-level experience of the frustrations of those working on development and a sensitivity to more critical arguments. Many Church professionals have come closer to, and have spent far more time wrestling with, poverty and its causes than Novak and his associates.

Moreover, it is clear today that leftist theorists about underdevelopment and development are far from doctrinaire. To an ever-increasing degree, Marxist-led governments are experimenting with market mechanisms and at least talking about opening space for an independent "civil society." Similarly, the mood among revolutionary organizations not in power and leftist theoreticians does not reflect the absolutism of some earlier periods.

Why is Novak so exercised to defend capitalism, when the

bishops' text contains no such attack—as even Novak himself sometimes acknowledges? Perhaps it is that despite the bishops' explicit acceptance of existing "economic arrangements," they raise questions of such magnitude that they point beyond present institutions. If so, it is not because crypto-socialists are manipulating unwitting bishops, but because Catholic social teaching provides a way for one to step out of customary ways of viewing things and in that—rather long-range—sense it is "subversive" of present institutions and their rationale. If that is so, Novak's instincts may be correct.

In closing this section we may briefly note Milton Friedman's critique of the bishops' letter, the thesis of which is aptly summed up in his title "Good Ends, Bad Means." Much of what Friedman says overlaps with Novak, but the tone is far more absolute. Thus he says that the bishops rely on government and make "warmed-over proposals that have been discredited by experience." "History speaks with one voice . . . : The most effective engine for improving the lot of the poor, the one method that has enabled low-income people to rise on the scale to become middle-income people, has been a free capitalist system and a free market. . . . Government policies are the major source of the residual poverty in the United States." That rather startling statement is buttressed by the assertion that poor schooling and the refusal to adopt voucher approaches to education handicap young people, who are further hindered by the minimum-wage law that prevents them from getting entry-level jobs.

Besides the bishops' policy proposals Friedman finds "repellant" the "collectivist moral strain that pervades the document." Rejecting the notion that a society or a country can have a duty, Friedman asserts the view that a country or a society is a "collection of individuals" and says that "only individuals can have moral obligations." "One cannot be compassionate by spending somebody else's money . . . the economy cannot do anything for or to people: it is a means whereby people do things for themselves or to or for one another. Only people can do things to people: only people can do things for people."

Friedman's critique is useful insofar as it expressly articulates a radically atomistic view of human nature. Many who disagree with his economics and policy prescriptions might nevertheless be hard pressed to refute him, since his individualism seems thoroughly American. This, it will be recalled, is the concern of *Habits of the Heart*: our main moral languages, which the authors call "instrumentalism" and "expressive individualism," are unable to provide a basis for solidarity. The bishops do not use the language of individualism but of persons-in-community, grounding it in Scripture, history, Church teaching, and what they see as the mainstream of a humanistic tradition.

RADICAL CRITIQUES

If *Economic Justice for All* prompts Novak to defend capitalism, others fault it precisely for its lack of a systemic analysis of capitalism. Lee Cormie has produced the most thorough such critique, while other commentaries have come from William Tabb, the Brazilian theologians Leonardo and Clodovis Boff, and William Murnion. (Although the Cormie and Tabb essays are based on the first draft of the letter, their observations apply to the final text as well.) The Center of Concern in Washington, D.C., while accepting the overall framework of the letter, also raised questions of a systemic nature.

The Boffs express a Third World disappointment:

> The system as such was not called into question. Once again capitalism has escaped being cursed. It can breathe freely. Without doubt, the American bishops strike vigorously at that apparatus; yet, they do so only in order to repair it and not to replace it. For them, capitalism "works," occasionally needing to be fixed and perfected.

Cormie faults the bishops for not making any "fundamental judgments concerning basic historical trends" and of thus being content to make a series of " 'empirical judgments' about specific issues, with little or no reflection on the relationships among them, or on the implications of the larger picture which emerges when considering them together."

Radical critics believe the bishops consistently shy away from conflict. For example, the bishops state that they do not regard the "option for the poor" as "adversarial." The Boffs believe that the biblical vision is conflictive, since the Bible sees the poor as those who are oppressed and need liberation.

Cormie also believes that this refusal to face up to conflict weakens the bishops document "theologically and biblically, morally and pastorally." Moreover, different interpretations of the world, different theoretical frameworks, reflect conflicts in society. Cormie discusses both the neoconservative theories fashionable in the mid-1980s and the older "liberal" perspective, which he sees as characteristic of the bishops' view. Consequently the authors of the document "are profoundly ambivalent about the performance of the American economy, apparently torn between their intention to be in solidarity with the victims and their hope that overcoming injustice will not provoke militant resistance from those with vested interests in the status quo, and conflict."

In contrast to both these trends, Cormie sees a growing number of critical analyses, which "reflect a more consistent effort to begin from the experience of poor and oppressed people."

In reviewing the bishops' figures on poverty, unemployment discrimination, and so forth, Cormie primarily faults the bishops for not making connections: for example, between inequalities of wealth and power, marginalization, and discrimination against racial minorities and women. Here, for example is part of his treatment of racism:

> Forced off the land by the mechanization of agriculture in the first decades of this century, [blacks] moved into the central cities at a time when industry was already decentralizing and moving. More recently, when good jobs in rapidly expanding corporate and government sectors increasingly demanded education, black children were attending deteriorating inner city schools. At a time when blacks, as

well as whites, increasingly need other social services, the flight of industry from Northeastern and Midwestern cities to the Southern rim of the U.S. and abroad undermines the ability of local governments to supply them. . . . [A]part from overt racism . . . the structures engendered in the processes of uneven capitalist development channel many Americans into undesirable, poor-paying jobs, and/or into outright poverty.

Like the Boffs, Cormie finds the bishops' document "exceptionally weak" on the world economy. The Boffs note that the bishops acknowledge dependence but that their overall rubric of interdependence makes them see poverty and wealth as standing side by side rather than in a causal relationship. They are especially indignant at the benign view of transnational corporations. Finally, the bishops attribute a "messianic function" to the United States, making it a "savior" of the Third World rather than the "culprit"—a "typical case of 'ideological inversion.' "

Without a comprehensive explanatory framework, the bishops are reduced to making moral appeals. Moreover, they seem to be appealing to the elites to undergo conversion rather than to the poor and disenfranchised to struggle for their rights. In fact, again say the Boffs, while they sound prophetic, raising their cry "in the heart of Babylon," "there is no indication 'against whom' " they are making their accusation. "There are no modern pharaohs, Acabs or Jeroboams in evidence." The bishops "attack sin generically without citing the sinner." What is lacking is a clear consciousness of "the structural dimension of morality."

William Tabb believes the letter can be given two readings. On the one hand, it can be seen as "historically progressive" and presented so as to be effective in an atmosphere that is "profoundly (if often unthinkingly) patriotic, favors individualistic solutions, and is hostile to the very word socialism." However, he also offers a less sympathetic viewpoint, namely, that the "institutional church is more a part of the problem than of the solution: that urging class collaboration and a moral economy within the capitalist frame of reference misspecifies both the reality of class and the defining characteristics of capitalism as a system." Tabb leans more toward the first interpretation, that is, he prefers to read the letter as a step in a process and the churches themselves as an "important arena of class struggle."

William Murnion, a philosopher who criticized the principles-to-application methodology of the peace pastoral (see page 13), sees the "more inductive and dialectical approach" of the economics pastoral as a great improvement. Nevertheless, he finds the bishops "more radical in theory than in practice." He believes that the "preferential option for the poor" is the key to the document and that Catholic social theology itself has shifted to a "socialist principle of justice." In a central part of his argument he compares the principle operative in four ideologies (libertarianism, liberalism, anarchism, socialism) in accordance with the way they conceive the relationship between people's contribution to the common good and the goods they receive from what is produced. Murnion uses variations on familiar slogans to encapsulate each ideology's principle of justice—libertarianism: "From each according to choice, to each according to merit"; liberalism: "From each according to ability, to each according to merit"; anarchism: "From each according to choice, to each according to need"; socialism: "From each according to ability, to each according to need." He concludes, "Of these four ideologies it is clearly socialism that is implicit in the American bishops' interpretation of the preferential option for the poor." This conclusion is buttressed with numerous paragraph references to the letter.

Ultimately, however, the document turns out revolutionary in theory but reformist in effect. Thus it functions as an "ideology" in Karl Mannheim's sense, that is, it masks the interests of a group. Since the Constitution does not provide for economic rights the same *warrant* it contains for civil rights, and since American culture is biased against programs that eradicate poverty, the poor "have but a remote or a debatable *entitlement* to the benefits implied by a preferential option for the poor." If the bishops want such an option, "they will have to help the poor to organize." Otherwise, the letter is "likely to foster only resignation in the poor, legitimizing rather than unmasking the injustice of American economic policy." Thus, despite the bishops' intentions, the letter serves the interests of the middle-class majority of their flocks.

Does Murnion really expect the bishops to recognize that their own principles are leading them in the direction of socialism? Similarly, do the Boffs expect the bishops to "name the beast"—capitalism—in a country where such language situates people outside the boundaries of political discourse? While I can understand the leftist concern for finding categories that can best reveal the way the economy works, I also find it unusual that the Boffs give the pope a benign reading, highlighting liberating motifs and downplaying or ignoring other strands in his thought, and yet are unwilling to take a similar hermeneutic tack with the U.S. bishops.

THE "IRON CAGE"

Both leftist and conservative critics object not only to particular conclusions but to the overall approach of the bishops. We now turn to some commentators more sympathetic to their execution, who nevertheless raise further questions. Some observers credit the bishops' moral earnestness but fault them for having failed to face squarely the depth of the present crisis and the resistance of institutions and culture.

Georgetown law professor Norman Birnbaum laments that the bishops

> tend to think in terms that were appropriate three decades ago when a social contract was possible (since a much higher proportion of workers were in unionized industry), when our domination of the world market was evident, and when full employment and a rising standard of living rendered the problem of poverty apparently soluble with our existing social technology. Now, real living standards are in decline in the

United States, full employment or anything like it seems impossible to attain and our political control of the world market is but partial. (155)

Birnbaum's Georgetown colleague, Victor Ferkiss, similarly raises unsettling questions about the present and the future of the American economy, questions that are no doubt latent in the letter but not given prominent attention. The bishops fail to face squarely the possibility that the American class structure is changing, being polarized into rich and poor. The bishops are "equivocal" in noting the reality of more women in the work force and a higher incidence of two-family incomes, while clinging to the notion that a single wage should be adequate to support a family. There is a growing underclass of people who are "not needed in the economy." Even organized labor increasingly accepts the presence of a poor class of cheap labor, especially immigrants, because without it even more jobs would be exported to other countries, leaving everyone worse off. Declining productivity per worker is an even more serious problem. Since a real decline in living standards means that one can no longer count on being better off in the future—"a radically new departure in American life"—it is not surprising that many people are hostile to redistributive schemes.

Ferkiss outlines some of the economic realities later brought to public attention by Peter G. Peterson. During the 1980s foreign investors were willing to lend to the United States to the point where the United States became a debtor nation. The time could come in which the United States would have to lower its standard of living by curtailing imports and radically increasing exports to pay—or even service—its debt. "[T]he handwriting is clearly on the wall. In many areas the United States is fighting for its economic survival." If the bishops' liberal assumptions about the possibilities of growth are erroneous, the problem of distribution becomes even more severe. Ferkiss sums up his reservations:

If . . . we are becoming a different kind of economy with a different kind of work force and a different class structure, with perhaps intractable problems of foreign and internal debt, a very different attitude toward economic possibility and personal security and a radically different position in the world economy, and if our economic problems are inextricably tied to our political problems, then most of the practical solutions put forth by the bishops are really not very useful, however desireable the ends they are intended to serve may be. What is really required is a fundamental change of attitude, toward which the bishops' letter does not clearly point.

Noting that the bishops fail "to address the question of power directly," Ferkiss states that as long as most Americans do not identify with the poor, however insecure they may feel, formal democracy is not the cure. Although a long-term "enlightenment of the citizenry is important, it is questionable how much the American public really wants or can endure."

Birnbaum also raises questions arising out of the tension between the bishops' ethical intentions and the resistance of culture and institutions. Although the bishops repeatedly ask people to consider the moral dimensions of their lives and decisions, they "underestimate the extent to which we are all prisoners of what Max Weber termed the 'iron cage,' the institutionally generated system of constraints that constitutes the organization of Western capitalism." The weakness of American unions, for example, has forced them to make concessions when forced with large-scale plant closures. Citing a number of European examples and studies, Birnbaum questions whether the bishops have put sufficient attention into considering how their ethical intentions should be realized programmatically.

The bishops, he says, "have done us a large favor by thinking countercyclically." Unfortunately, they do not distinguish sufficiently the analytic and prophetic dimensions of their thought. Moreover, by emphasizing the preferential option for the poor, they tend to moralize and fail to appeal sufficiently to self-interest. Their intuition of an inner impoverishment and a lower quality of life can provide the basis for a "coalition uniting the poor and the ostensibly privileged." The letter's proposal for a new American experiment ignores the fact that it took much time and conflict, including the Civil War, to consolidate political rights. The bishops are accused of thinking "ahistorically, making suggestions that resemble an unconnected list of proposals rather than a coherent program."

Birnbaum seems to be saying that the bishops' effort to focus on ethical concerns and to give only hints at how they might be embodied fails, because it does not take seriously enough the fact that there is a morality already embodied in institutions. At various points he refers to the "fabrication" of morality by the media. In one sharp formulation, he asks, "Have the institutions the bishops seek to change so shaped humans to their measure that their moral and factual identification with capitalism precludes major changes?"

LIBERAL OR COMMUNITARIAN?

Some critics have derided the liberal policy proposals put forward in *Economic Justice for All* as warmed-over "Great Society" ideas. Such a reading seems superficial, however; the letter makes appeal to other kinds of reasoning and seems to point beyond present institutions.

Are the bishops "liberals" in the older, more historical and more philosophical sense? As is well known, the Catholic church has only partially assimilated the liberal tradition; its ties to the peasantry and monarchy kept it hostile to capitalism and modern Western institutions for centuries, and a reconciliation was only formalized at Vatican II. Indeed, one of Michael Novak's central contentions is that the Catholic church still has much to learn and assimilate from the liberal tradition. For example, he sees it as symptomatic that the letter gravitates toward values of "solidarity" rather than to those of "pluralism" and "liberty."

Hence there arise a series of questions: what is the "language" of the letter? What is the relationship between "Catholic social teaching" and philosophical liberalism? Is the letter a sign that the Catholic church still does not appreciate the genius of liberalism? Or does it provide a critical corrective to the liberalism that so surrounds us that we scarcely notice it? Here we may again mention the concern voiced in *Habits of the Heart* that having almost lost their "biblical" and "republican" languages, ordinary Americans are unable to explain their lives except in terms of individual preferences that have no ulterior justification.

David Hollenbach, a Jesuit theologian specializing in social ethics, who served as a consultant to the drafting committee, has sought to clarify the question of where the letter fits into the contemporary debate in a paper titled "Liberalism, Communitarianism and the Bishops' Pastoral Letter on the Economy." Noting that there is a renewed discussion among theoreticians of liberalism, he lists four assumptions common to liberals: First, every person has a right to equal concern and respect. Second, society should be organized fairly. Third, the pluralism of convictions about what constitutes the human good excludes any imposition of a comprehensive vision of that good. Fourth, society should intervene to counteract the impact of unfair advantages of some over others.

Out of the conviction that liberalism is incapable of dealing with the problems of modern society and indeed that it rests on an erroneous individualistic and ahistorical conception of the self, there has grown an alternate communitarian conception, proposed by critics such as Alasdair MacIntyre and Michael Sandel. Hollenbach similarly synthesizes their common principles (which I summarize at slightly greater length because they are less familiar): First, the human person is essentially a social being; social bonds are constitutive of one's selfhood. Second, how persons should live depends on the kinds of relationships valued as good in themselves. Third, human beings do not know the good spontaneously but must be schooled in virtue, learning from a community tradition. Fourth, how society should be organized depends on a vision of the common good; since the pluralism of modern life frustrates such a vision, however, we must concentrate on learning virtues in smaller communities, which can share a vision of the common good. MacIntyre's comparison of such communities to the early Benedictine monasteries indicates his drastic view of how "dark" the present age is.

The communitarian critique should not be mistaken for conventional conservatism. From a communitarian perspective, both liberalism and conservatism in their more usual meanings share a deep-seated individualism.

Classical Catholic social teaching obviously expresses communitarian themes. Where does *Economic Justice for All* stand? Is it too little appreciative of liberalism, too communitarian, as Novak might argue? Or has it been too accommodating to liberalism, as others fear?

In Hollenbach's view, the letter is committed *both* to the dignity of all persons *and* "to a strongly communitarian understanding of what it is to be a person." He finds that the letter "blends" both vocabularies. Hollenbach would seem to regard the primary language as communitarian, since he sees liberal language introduced to impose restraints on the communitarian vision of the good society. In part, this is because the letter has the realism to recognize the danger that some might seek to impose their particular good over others under the guise of the common good.

Invoking John Courtney Murray, Hollenbach emphasizes the letter's distinction between public order and the common good. That distinction is rooted in the fact that society is more comprehensive than the state. "Public order" is understood to embrace conditions for communal life based on mutual respect: justice, public peace, public morality (based on the existing consensus), and public prosperity. The quest for justice, which citizens pursue as citizens, is part of a larger whole, the quest for the common good.

The pastoral letter achieves a "synthesis" between liberalism and communitarianism, not by splitting the difference, as though they were two alternate social theories but by seeing them as relevant to different domains: "the liberal theory of justice and rights to the political order, and the communitarian vision of the common good to the rest of social activity."

Hollenbach emphasizes that the bishops' understanding of justice as participation is richer than that of liberals, such as John Rawls. The opposite of participation is marginalization, whether political or economic. Thus the bishops expand the liberal concern for political rights to the economic sphere. The letter "argues that all persons have rights not only to the conditions necessary for political cooperation or participation, but to the basic conditions to be participants in the economic and social sphere as well." Hollenbach summarizes:

> The letter embodies a moral theory that defends the liberal commitment to pluralism in the institutional life of society. It also urges the cultivation of the virtues needed to move society toward the realization of its full conception of the common good. At the same time it presses beyond the classical liberalism that communitarian critics find thin, deracinated, and an inadequate response to the anomie and disillusionment with public life that is very much around us. (26)

In the "Message" that accompanied the letter the bishops recognized that "men and women of good will may disagree" with them on "specific points" and said that they expected a "fruitful exchange among differing viewpoints." While they seemed to expect agreement over general principles and some measure of disagreement over policy recommendations, this chapter indicates that a good deal of the discussion has dealt with principles, or perhaps with what philosophers call "middle axioms."

Wide disagreement about underlying principles is itself a fact of our situation. We won't find the "answers" by arguing but by experimenting and struggling.

· 6 ·

BRINGING IT HOME

A s I was beginning this book, a nationally known pacifist priest stayed overnight at a Philadelphia parish. When the pastor asked him if he would be available for discussion about the letters, he replied, "I really haven't thought about them much at all." When I interviewed a sister who does community organizing in a black neighborhood and is also a pillar in the Catholic Peace Fellowship, I got a similar reaction. While she appreciates what the bishops have done and perhaps feels validated by it, she has not spent much time with the texts themselves.

Some months after the final version of the letter on the economy was published, a *National Catholic Reporter* poll found that 71 percent of adult Catholics questioned indicated that they had never heard of it. In conversation with my own family (including in-laws, about fifteen family units, almost all Catholics), the topic of the letters has never risen spontaneously. In church I do not recall the letters being invoked in a Sunday sermon more than once or twice.

We have already noted that both letters received considerable attention when initially released, and they have received respectful attention in academic conferences and journals. However, they will have little long-run impact in our society unless they are implemented within the Catholic church itself. Will they remain an exercise of the bishops, their staffs, and a narrow Catholic intelligentsia? Or can Church leaders find ways to bring the letters into the ongoing life of parishes and Church institutions?

Even given a willingness to attempt systematic implementation, other questions can be raised. Will the Catholic church even observe them in its own institutions? Won't most Catholic lay people feel free to disregard these letters as they have other hierarchical pronouncements (birth control, for example)? How can a Church that is so conservative on social matters (the role of women, sexuality, and especially abortion, homosexuality, and AIDS education) be so liberal on matters of domestic and foreign policy? What about recent Vatican moves to stifle dissent (disciplining of pacifist Archbishop Raymond Hunthausen of Seattle, firing of Father Charles Curran from Catholic University in Washington, D.C., and the Vatican pressures against the signers of a *New York Times* ad urging that Church authorities recognize that there exists in the Church a diversity of viewpoints on abortion?)

Although some of these questions are only indirectly related to the pastoral letters, they all have some bearing either on the Church's credibility or on its ability to move from words to action. In this chapter, then, we will look at some of these questions as they relate to the pastoral letters.

LIBERAL POSITIONS FROM A CONSERVATIVE CHURCH?

If one assumes that political and religious attitudes tend to correlate, it is logical enough to situate Catholicism toward the rightward end of the spectrum that extends from fundamentalist

Christians to secularized leftist radicals. In that case, the positions adopted by the bishops in their letters seem to be curiously distant from their base.

However true such a correlation might have been a generation ago or more, it is not true today. Any observer of the Central America movement of the 1980s, for example, must be aware that religiously motivated people are often more in evidence than the secular left.

Sociologist Stephen Hart has investigated the relationship between religious belief and political position. Through in-depth interviews of several hours each with fifty individuals, he found that individual believers could invoke Christian themes to support both conservative and liberal—and even radical—attitudes in social and economic areas. Moreover, these attitudes could vary on matters of both substance (what kind of society should we have?) and procedure (how should we move in that direction?).

Similarly, a September 1987 Gallup poll commissioned by the Times-Mirror Publishing Company concluded that "contrary to conventional wisdom, deep religious faith (or evangelicalism or 'born-again' Christianity) is not simply a phenomenon of the political right." The study, which sought to deal with "the growing imprecision in the very language of politics and public opinion," concluded that traditional categories (Democrat/Republican, liberal/conservative) were no longer accurate indicators of voting behavior. Three of the eleven categories of the study's proposed new typology ("the New Dealers, '60s Democrats, and the Partisan Poor") were both solidly Democratic and as religiously committed as those the researchers called "the Moralists." Together these three categories constitute 28 percent of the adult population and 35 percent of the likely electorate.

The important thing to note is that religious belief can combine with social and political liberalism and conservatism in different manners. Thus, "Moral Republicans" (who voted 97 percent for Reagan in 1984) are conservative both socially and politically; "New Deal Democrats" (older, often Catholic, and blue-collar, who voted 30 percent for Reagan) are politically liberal and socially conservative; while " '60s Democrats" (well educated, often married women with children, who voted 25 percent for Reagan) are liberal both socially and politically. For the sake of comparison we may note that one of the survey categories was "Seculars," who are "heavily concentrated on the East and West coasts, professional, 11% Jewish," who make up 8 percent of the adult population and 9 percent of the likely electorate, who in the 1986 congressional election voted 72 percent Democratic.

These general observations may pave the way for some observations on Catholics. Examining numerous surveys taken over a twenty-year period, Andrew Greeley sharply criticizes stereotypes of Catholics as conservatives. He summarizes his findings; "On virtually every measure of social and political and racial attitudes Catholics occupy a middle position between Jews and Protestants—a little bit left of center." The following chart summarizes research on attitudes toward spending priorities:

	PROTESTANTS	CATHOLICS	JEWS
Think *too little money* is spent on:		(percentage)	
ENVIRONMENT	54	63	66
HEALTH	56	64	74
CITIES	45	55	76
EDUCATION	52	55	73
WEAPONS	25	19	11

Greeley finds similar figures on issues such as gun control, civil liberties, and racial integration.

Although Catholics as a group have risen educationally and economically in recent decades, they retain their traditional loyalty to the Democratic party. Although there was a slight de-alignment from the party among Catholics in the 1970s (as there was among Protestants), about 55 percent of Catholics still describe themselves as Democrats and three-fifths "regardless of what they say their political affiliation is, routinely vote for Democratic congressional and senatorial candidates."

If Catholics as a whole are "a little bit left of center" in the American political spectrum, the pastoral letters are not the product of Church leaders isolated from the people in the pews. Indeed, the bishops may be articulating what many Catholics, though by no means all, either instinctively feel or are ready to hear. Of course to be "a little left of center" does not necessarily mean being open to raising the fundamental questions that periodically surface in both letters.

Greeley found astonishing evidence of the impact of the peace pastoral. In the course of his career—as a wide-ranging sociologist, theologian, social and political commentator, and in recent years, novelist—he has found himself increasingly estranged from many sectors of the Catholic community, including both what he calls the "Catholic liberal/left/peace-and-justice crowd" and many bishops. In his mind, they are too fixed in their own ideas to study and respect the data as he does. In particular their images of ordinary Catholics are formed more by stereotypes than by competent research. In 1984 he turned to examine Catholic attitudes on peace and war, fully expecting to find that the pastoral letter had "bombed." To his surprise he found that 54 percent of Catholics now thought too much money was being spent on defense—a jump up from 32 percent the previous year—while the figure for Protestants had remained unchanged at that same percentage.

He surmised that the bishops had hit upon the moment when many Americans were becoming uneasy about the Reagan buildup and the growing danger of nuclear war. "The stand of the bishops, at just the right time (mostly a matter of good fortune), provided for uneasy Catholics a focus for their concern which was not available to Protestants." He further surmised that it was not the text of the document that focused the change but the discussion of the pastoral in the media.

Certainly the bishops' aim in writing the letters was not simply to tilt Catholic opinion in a particular direction, nor should the letters' impact be judged simply on shifts in Catholic opinions as detected in polls. In both letters the bishops see themselves as at the beginning of a long process. Or as Father Marvin Boes of the Peace and Justice Committee of Sioux City, Iowa, put it, "It took five years to put the document together so it will take us some time to implement it."

IMPLEMENTATION EFFORTS

In *The Challenge of Peace* the bishops say, "we urge every diocese and parish to implement balanced and objective educational programs to help people at all age levels to understand better the issues of war and peace." Such programs "must receive a high priority during the next several years" (280).

For follow-up to the letter three bishops were appointed to serve as an oversight committee. A priest and a Catholic laywoman were chosen to staff an office, soon called the Pastoral Letter Clearinghouse. For one year this office provided study guides, videotapes, and short brochures on the pastoral and published a bulletin. No comprehensive study of implementation efforts was carried out, and thus information is anecdotal, according to Catherine Inez Adelsic, on the office staff. Here is a sampling of what is known about some implementation efforts:

- Typically, diocesan offices trained people from parishes to lead discussions. For example in the diocese of Little Rock, Arkansas, an estimated 50 percent of the parishes held some kind of activity.

- The diocese of Bridgeport, Connecticut, first held meetings with parish leaders and then a series of four to five talks at parishes, with an average of twenty to thirty people in attendance. In a second phase the diocese sought to move beyond a study model to one more oriented to action.

- Military personnel were particularly active in parish discussions. Some were bewildered at what the bishops had done and others were hostile. Discussion of what the bishops had actually said, including specific references to the military, seemed to defuse some of these reactions. The peace pastoral has been incorporated into some military courses (for example, at the Air War College at Maxwell Air Force Base in Alabama). Military chaplains also gave workshops on the letter.

- Around the country there were numerous conferences, symposiums, and study days on the letter.

- Catholic educational systems in particular made use of the letter. In response to a spring 1983 letter from the Association of Catholic Colleges and Universities (ACCU) some 140 institutions said they would make the letter a topic of study and reflection during 1983–84 and would designate a coordinator of activities of that kind. The entire December 1983 *Momentum*, the journal of the National Catholic Educational Association, was devoted to the letter. The issue contained seventeen articles and an equal number of shorter accounts. The writers were not simply restating the themes of the letter but raising educational questions (e.g., an article "Can a Catholic Military School Promote Justice and Peace?") and describing educational experiences (e.g., "Teaching Hiroshima—Thinking About the Unthinkable"). Several articles dealt with psychological issues and processes, such as conflict resolution in the classroom.

When they said that their own criteria require "continual public scrutiny of what our government proposes to do with the deterrent" (CP, 187), the bishops implicitly committed themselves to some kind of follow-up assessment—all the more so since their letter did not deal with the SDI ("Star Wars"), which was announced in 1983. A statement they debated and approved in June 1988 reiterated the major themes of the 1983 letter. They welcomed the seemingly changing relationship between the United States and the USSR and advocated ratification of the INF agreement as well as progress toward "deep cuts" in strategic weapons. Most of the long (sixteen thousand words) document was a restatement of the principles of the 1983 letter. If it was read closely, one could deduce that the bishops were highly skeptical of SDI on grounds of technical feasibility and cost. Since SDI has often been defended as morally superior to deterrence—its defensive "shield" would supposedly make offensive weapons and retaliatory deterrence obsolete—the bishops seek to "dispel the notion that the moral character of SDI can be decided in terms of . . . intentions." However, rather than rejecting it as a fantasy and a boondoggle for defense industries that would further distort the nation's priorities, they respectfully say it "should be maintained as a research and development program within the restraints of the ABM treaty." Pax Christi voiced the concerns of Catholic peace activists when it criticized the draft as "embarrassingly secular," indecisive, "lengthy, heavy, technical reading," and "disappointing." In short, the bishops reiterated their 1983 positions but broke no new ground.

Perhaps judging that they had not put sufficient resources into the follow-up to the peace pastoral, the bishops set up an implementation office for the economics pastoral and a budget of $525,000 for three years of operation. This office also functions primarily as a clearinghouse of information about what is being done around the country. In the letter itself the bishops had urged

> Renewed emphasis on Catholic social teaching in our schools, colleges and universities; special seminars with corporate officials, union leaders, legislators, bankers and the like; the organization of small groups composed of people from different ways of life to meditate together on the Gospel and ethical norms; speakers' bureaus; family programs; clearinghouses of available material; pulpit aids for priests; diocesan television and radio programs; research projects in our universities.(360)

The following examples give some idea of the kinds of activities and programs arising directly out of *Economic Justice for All:*

- By October 1987 some 123,000 copies of the letter had been distributed (primarily sold) (plus 5,000 copies of a Spanish translation); in addition 87,000 copies of a summary, 4,500 copies of a study guide, and 450 diocesan implementation manuals had also been distributed.

- There have been numerous efforts to make the letter, written at a college freshman level, accessible to a wider audience: 935,000 copies of a four-page summary were distributed; at least 600 video presentations in several forms are circulating; a four-member Chicago-based troupe called Between the Times has traveled to a number of dioceses to present a musical/dramatic version of the letter.

- Early in the process the office organized a nationwide live satellite hookup that permitted diocesan-level groups to see and hear presentations by experts on the themes of the pastoral as well as by organizers and to phone in queries. By taping the conference they had an educational resource ready to use.

- Shortly after the publication of the pastoral, the nine bishops of Maryland issued their own letter, applying the themes of the letter to their state. The letter was released at a press conference held in a Baltimore soup kitchen. The major headings are taxes, poverty, housing, and unemployment. "For one in seven Maryland families," say the bishops, "home means a dwelling with no indoor plumbing, a hot-plate for a kitchen, a leaky roof, walls flaking deadly lead-based paint, windows stuffed with newspapers, faulty wiring, rats and roaches." Under each major heading the bishops make recommendations for public policy as well as exhortations to the private sector and individuals. At one point the bishops took the governor of

Maryland through some Baltimore slums in an effort to persuade him to devote some windfall state tax revenues to programs for the poor. That effort was said to have been successful.

· Eight months after the establishment of the implementation office, coordinators of implementation had been appointed in 130 dioceses (out of a total of approximately 178). Most had set up task forces, and over half had implementation plans. The general pattern has been to incorporate the letter into ongoing programs, such as clergy education, teacher training, and lay leadership formation. A third of the dioceses were reported to be working with nonchurch organizations or coalitions, such as the Poor Peoples' Campaign, welfare reform coalitions, and self-help credit unions.

· At their 1987 annual meeting 150 delegates of the National Federation of Priests' Councils, held in Saint Paul, Minnesota, made the economic pastoral their theme. This federation is the main opportunity for the voicing of priests' concerns within the Church in the United States. Questions of wealth and poverty seemed to predominate. Some expressed concern over middle-class Catholics who might feel the Church was turning against them. There were proposals for linking parishes of rich and poor, not only for financial assistance but also to share lives. Resolutions urged that Church bodies exemplify the spirit of the letter "by ensuring just work practices among all employees of the Church, including the right to organize and bargain collectively and fairly through the institution of their own choice." Many delegates seemed to see the role of the priest as "prophetic," even if that means alienating the privileged.

· In June 1987 the Association of Catholic Colleges and Universities sponsored a conference on the letter at Loyola Marymount University in Los Angeles for professors and campus ministers from around the country. A major point of discussion was how to integrate Church social teaching into curricula. Interdisciplinary approaches were put forward and existing models shared and discussed.

• The Office of Implementation and RENEW, a national program of biblically based spiritual formation existing in eighty dioceses, began to collaborate. The RENEW program, which utilizes small group discussion meetings in homes over a three-year period, has been a vital force in Catholicism. The collaboration between the two programs means that materials and themes from the economic pastoral will be integrated into a program of spiritual growth at the local level.

• In Erie, Pennsylvania, clergy and business people who had already been meeting for two years agreed to focus their discussions for fall 1987 on documents on the economy issued by the Presbyterian, Lutheran, Methodist, and Catholic churches.

One of the few efforts thus far to integrate both pastoral letters is *The Pastorals on Sundays*, a collection of paragraph-length passages from both letters for all Sundays of the year, keyed into the themes of the liturgical readings. The booklet is intended as a preaching aid to enable priests to weave selections or themes from the pastorals into their sermons. The selections are mainly from passages related to the area of spirituality or the larger principles of peace and justice rather than those devoted to policy questions. Connections are suggestive: for example, when the gospel account is of Jesus walking on the water toward the apostles in the midst of a storm, the proposed passage from the economics pastoral quotes the bishops as saying that "we cannot be frightened by the magnitude and complexity" of our economic problems, and the selection from the peace pastoral urges that with regard to U.S.-USSR relations we must not "underestimate . . . our human potential for creative diplomacy and God's action in our midst which can open the way to changes we could barely imagine." Thus, a preacher might evoke the disciples' encounter with Jesus on the lake and then draw parallels with the kind of "storms" the hearers might encounter in personal and family life as well as in the larger public world, deftly incorporating a few phrases from the pastoral letters. If this were done consistently, over a period of time Catholics would become familiar with the spirit and major themes of the letters.

In fact, however, it seems clear that thus far the pastoral letters are not invoked very frequently from Catholic pulpits. A survey undertaken by the diocese of Richmond, Virginia, found that three years after its publication only 10 percent of the respondents had become familiar with the peace pastoral through the pulpit. Thirty percent said their source was the media, and a surprising 27 percent said they had read the document or a summary. Another 30 percent said they were not familiar with the document.

This survey reveals the major stumbling block to widespread familiarity with the pastorals among Catholics: the nature of the Catholic parish and the role of the parish priest. Although parish councils have been introduced in many places in the last two decades, the pastor is still in charge. If the parish priest does not take the initiative, it is unlikely that ordinary Catholics will come in contact with the bishops' documents. Many priests apparently do not feel comfortable preaching on complex issues such as deterrence or social policy. Others oppose the bishops' findings or feel they have overstepped their authority. Some fear the resistance of their parishioners. Some priests who take leadership are not supported by their diocese. The fact that the letters have relatively little impact at the parish level might also indicate that many priests feel overwhelmed by their normal routine or do not see peace and justice concerns as central to their ministry.

Furthermore, the tradition of adult Catholic education is weak or almost nonexistent in Catholic parishes, as contrasted with many Protestant denominations, in which adult classes are a normal feature of congregational life. Thus the typical Catholic parishioner's involvement is Sunday mass. Other parish activities include catechism for children and young adolescents, a parish school, prayer groups, clubs for young people and senior citizens, perhaps charitable activity—but few ready-made forums for the kind of questions raised in the pastoral letters.

As we have seen, both letters have been incorporated into Catholic education, especially at the college level. Educators raise serious questions, however. One of the most important is how the concerns of the letters are to be integrated. Should it be in the form of interdisciplinary programs in which students could major or minor in peace studies or justice issues? Should there be course requirements in these areas? One writer points out that simply adding such a course requirement might entail the hiring of many extra teachers and costs (perhaps $200,000 a year at Catholic University of America and $500,000 at Notre Dame). Or should the letters be worked into courses in economics, political science, theology, and so forth? What, then, becomes of academic freedom and especially the claim to value-free education? Or should Catholic institutions be unabashedly committed to a values orientation?

What does "implementation" actually mean? Most of the efforts described here assume an educational model of implementation: the bishops have spoken and now the task is to bring their message to the people, who will then, it is hoped, put it into practice in their innumerable life decisions.

Such a model runs the risk of seeing the people's role in a rather passive light, that of accepting an already prepared teaching. Suppose, however, the focus is not primarily on coming to understand and accept the bishops' *texts* and their conclusions but on coming to grips with the issues in a process similar to theirs. Thus, Catholics and Catholic groups would struggle with the issues of nuclear weapons, deterrence policy, unemployment, rising poverty, the farm crisis, the debt crisis, and so forth, using the letters as aids. Their primary *text*, however, would not be the letters as such but rather the present situation in the world, as best it can be understood. The aim would be to become *engaged* as the bishops did, to wrestle with the perplexities and seek to move to action, however imperfect might be their understanding.

In fact, some Catholic agencies and organizations prefer to work on what might be called an empowerment model, as contrasted with an adult-education model. Thus, rather than seeking to stimulate the formation of discussion groups in parishes, they strive to help people deal with their problems and struggle for their rights, either in existing organizations or by forming new ones. In Houma-Thibodaux, Louisiana, an area in deep depression because of falling oil prices, for example, Catholic organizations work with the ecumenical Alternative Development Task Force setting up food banks, helping people find jobs, and encouraging small-business development. In 1986 Catholic Social Services founded the Coalition to Restore Coastal Louisiana to pressure for action to save the wetlands that are vanishing due to erosion and thus severely harming the local fishing industry. The Church was rewording the agricultural section of the economics pastoral in terms of Louisiana, where "farming means fishing and soil means wetlands."

Finally it should be noted that there are already Catholic organizations, both official and unofficial, that were "implementing" the letters years before they were conceived. Since its inauguration in late 1969, the Campaign for Human Development (CHD), sponsored by the bishops, has aided local groups with small grants. The $10 million annual budget is small—it represents only about twenty cents per Catholic. CHD monies have generally gone to local groups, such as cooperatives or community organizations. Some groups are engaged primarily in advocacy (e.g., the South Carolina Coalition Against the Death Penalty), but most have an economic component, (e.g., the Dungannon Sewing Cooperative in Virginia). More recently, CHD has been moving to aid dioceses become actors in regional economic issues. Thus the focus is not only on individual worker-run enterprises but on regional approaches to economic development. The experience of parishes and dioceses at the local level can be seen in *Economic Justice for All*, especially when it deals with plant closings and the need for broad-based regional planning.

In 1971 Catholic sisters set up Network as a "Catholic social justice lobby." The organization, whose activists are largely sisters, advises its members on pending legislation in areas such as housing, welfare reform, economic equality for women, full employment, arms control, disarmament, the debt crisis, Central America, and southern Africa. Network's lobbying on policy questions that have moral dimensions is essentially a grass-roots effort. It may be noted that the bishops themselves frequently lobby by giving testimony in congressional hearings.

More like a think-tank is the Center of Concern, a Jesuit-initiated group, also in Washington, D.C. Center activities include preparing studies on current issues and long-range trends from within the tradition of Catholic social teaching and conducting seminars and workshops for religious groups around the country. The Center of Concern prepared critiques of the drafts of both pastoral letters as well as follow-up educational materials for use in parishes and Catholic institutions.

Such organizations are a reminder that the letters were not born by episcopal spontaneous generation, but were in fact the outgrowth of activities taking place throughout American Catholicism. The "implementation" of the letters should be seen not as a fresh beginning but as the intensification of processes already underway.

CHURCH INSTITUTIONS

In *Economic Justice for All* the bishops had said that the Church itself should follow the norms and principles applicable to any economic endeavor and that indeed it should be "exemplary." To put that into perspective, in my own city of Philadelphia, beginning teachers earn $12,300 a year at a Catholic elementary school and $13,550 at an archdiocesan high school. Both are considerably below the $17,638 starting rate in Philadelphia public schools, and the gap widens with experience. Moreover, under Cardinal John Krol the Church steadfastly resisted unionization efforts. Pay scales in Catholic schools and other institutions have tended to be lower than the prevailing rates. Moreover, Catholic institutions have not completely overcome the legacy of clerical autocracy.

In closing their November 1986 critique William Simon and Michael Novak make a plea for "economic justice for nuns," calling it a "scandal" that, facing a pensionless old age, some sisters have to turn to the state for assistance. On this point their most resolute adversaries will agree. Since many younger sisters have left religious life and few young women enter, the median age of sisters is now sixty-four. In the coming years the Church— out of justice to women who have given it their life—will have to raise substantial funds to help them meet their needs. The bishops have approved the beginning of a special fund, and other efforts are underway.

These examples make it clear that applying the prescriptions of *Economic Justice for All* to the Church's internal workings will carry a price tag. Commenting on the economics pastoral, Bishop William McManus (retired from Fort Wayne) says that the general guidelines need to be spelled out more. He raises a number of questions about what constitutes a just wage and then suggests as a rule of thumb that a minimum starting salary "for any church employed professional holding a college degree and otherwise qualified and certified should be four hundred dollars a week." With 5 percent annual raises, a ten-year employee would earn six hundred dollars a week. He suggests a similar arrangement for "paraprofessionals, semiprofessionals and others employed full time," starting at three hundred dollars a week.

Such proposals would demand greater revenues, that is, higher contributions from Catholics. In fact, Bishop McManus makes his observations in a work he coauthored with Andrew Greeley on Catholic contributions to the Church. Greeley's major finding is that today Catholics contribute an average of $328 a year to the Church, as opposed to American Protestant contributions averaging $580—despite the fact that on the average Catholics earn $27,500 a year, more than a thousand dollars higher than Protestant earnings ($26,400). Since the 1960s Catholic contributions have declined in percentage terms, while Protestant contributions have remained steady. If Catholics contributed like Protestants, Church income would increase from $6 billion to $12.7 billion. That would enable the Church to pay just wages and carry out other activities. However, to do so, the Church would have to modernize its fundraising practices and practice accountability to contributors.

It is only in recent times that the question of just employment practices within the Church has been raised systematically. For example, in 1986 the National Association of Church Personnel Administrators (in other words, managers, clerical and lay) have published guidelines on matters such as clearly delineated personnel policies, participatory decision making, affirmative action, personnel development, grievance procedures, and so forth. Partly in response to the economics pastoral, the archdiocese of Los Angeles initiated a process to review salaries and benefits of Church employees in order to make them more just and more uniform, starting with archdiocesan offices and agencies before moving to parishes and schools.

A "SEAMLESS GARMENT"?

Many are undoubtedly puzzled that the bishops can be quite liberal politically and so conservative on matters of social policy related to sexuality (birth control, homosexuality, and especially abortion). The bishops, on the other hand, see their own position as quite consistent and fault what they see as the inconsistency in others. In their programmatic 1976 pastoral letter "To Live in Christ Jesus," the bishops begin with theological statements about Jesus Christ and go on to consider moral questions related to the family, the nation, and the community of nations. In this framework they consider such questions as the indissolubility of marriage, contraception, premarital and extramarital sex, homosexuality, euthanasia, abortion, women's rights, racial justice, North-South relations, conscientious objection, nuclear weapons, and human rights. This document and numerous others demonstrate that the 1983 and 1986 pastoral letters largely restate and further develop positions the bishops have already taken. Furthermore, some bishops believe the effort to influence public policy on peace and economic issues is an outgrowth of their earlier efforts to influence policy on "pro-life" issues.

In *The Challenge of Peace* the bishops speak of violence taking "many faces": oppression, violation of human rights, economic and sexual exploitation, and so forth. "Abortion in particular blunts a sense of the sacredness of human life. In a society where the innocent unborn are killed wantonly, how can we expect people to feel righteous revulsion at the act of war or threat of killing noncombatants in war?" They then acknowledge that many join them in their opposition to war but part ways from them in their "no to war on innocent human life in the womb." They find the 15 million abortions carried out in the United States since 1973 "symptoms of a kind of disease of the human spirit." Mentioning current discussions of infanticide, euthanasia, and the involvement of physicians in carrying out the death penalty, they plead "with all who would work to end the scourge of war to begin by defending life at its most defenseless, the life of the unborn" (285–89).

Beginning in 1983 Cardinal Bernardin gave a number of lectures on the "consistent ethic of life," or the "seamless garment," as it is sometimes called. He and the bishops were arguing for an across-the-board reverence for life, challenging those on one side to defend fetal life and those on the other to extend their concern for the unborn to the arms race, capital punishment, and economic justice. The bishops were joined by many Catholic pacifists who have a horror of abortion. This stand has been embodied in groups calling themselves Pro-Lifers for Survival.

Although a full treatment would take us far from the two pastoral letters, we should pay some attention to what the bishops call a "consistent ethic of life," because they see it as the cornerstone of their approach. We will consider what questions they raise about consistency, the connections they make between Catholic stances on abortion and attitudes toward sexuality and women, and finally the question of Church authority itself.

In their own minds, the consistent ethic of life makes eminent sense. Is it sociologically realistic, however, to expect many people to accept a "seamless garment" approach? Kristin Luker's study of pro-life and pro-choice activists finds them so far apart on their whole constellation of values that the groups seemingly have virtually nothing in common (although 80 percent of the activists on both sides are women). As Rosemary Ruether crisply summarizes the differences Luker found,

> Pro-life women believe that men and women are fundamentally different. Women's first and primary role is marriage and motherhood, and women should work only if they are not married or do not have children. They regard morality as fixed and eternally given by God. Pro-choice women, on the other hand, see men and women as similar and believe that they should be able to play similar public roles in society. Childbearing is a primary hindrance to women's equality in society, and highly effective birth control that allows women either to have no children or to plan when and how many children they will have is, therefore, essential. Abortion is necessary as a backup. . . . For pro-choice women, morality is not fixed or divinely revealed. It is instead a function of rationality and should aim at the optimization of human potential.

These are descriptions of the activist minorities, not of the American majority. What they indicate, however, is that there are few points of contact between the values of those most committed to the abortion debate on either side. While Luker examines attitudes toward women's role and does not consider how these values correlate with attitudes toward war, peace, and economic justice, they seem to indicate that there will be a deep gulf between most antiabortion activists and most peace activists. Thus it is hard to see either side accepting a "consistent life ethic" in the bishops' sense; sociologically, it seems to be a will-of-the-wisp.

Moreover, the bishops' claim to consistency does not go unchallenged. Sister Joan Chittister believes that the bishops undercut their own credibility when they "claim that nuclear destruction and policy are repugnant to them but say it is impossible to be morally absolute in their repudiation of the manufacture or use of nuclear weapons because there is enough need for deterrence and enough doubt about their effects to command their toleration." The bishops "show no such hesitation or ambivalence about abortion. In that case they draw universal and absolute implications with ease," applying them to Catholic hospitals, Catholic doctors, and Catholic monies. Noting that the arguments for abortion are the same, she asks,

> What is a woman to think: That when life is in the hands of a woman, then to destroy it is always morally wrong, never to be condoned, always a grave and universal evil? But when life is in the hands of men, millions of lives at one time, all life at one time, then destruction can be theologized and some people's needs and lives can be made more important than other people's needs and lives?

Her idea of consistency would be that the bishops be as forthright on deterrence as they are about abortion.

Consistency can cut both ways. In an article titled "To Make A Seamless Garment, Use a Single Piece of Cloth," Christine Gudorf contrasts the official approach to war to the approach on abortion, especially in the type of reasoning used. She believes the bishops fail to take women seriously and see them only in biological terms. There is a glaring contrast, she believes, between the bishops' pressing for legislation on abortion and their failure to do so on war, where they "rely on persuasion."

> When the Church recognizes that abortion is as complex, as social, and as conflictive of rights as the issues of war or hunger, then perhaps we, the Church, can address abortion

with more evenhanded compassion and war and hunger with even more rigor.

I second Cardinal Bernardin's call for a consistent ethic of life, a "seamless garment." But. . . . [w]e will never convince those involved in the taking of one and a half million aborted lives a year to consider the life of the unborn reverently if we do not evince reverence for the mothers of those unborn, for the starving millions of our world, the hundreds of thousands of innocent civilians threatened by death in war.

In surveying positions taken by Catholic moralists on abortion, one finds that the great divide is between what might be called absolutists and nonabsolutists. For some, any abortion is in itself a serious sin because it is the taking of human life. Most of those who hold such a position will base it on a combination of natural-law-type arguments bolstered by appeals to tradition and Church authority. A minority would hold a "consistent life ethic." Across the divide among what could be called nonabsolutists would stand many moral theologians who believe abortion may be a moral choice under restrictive conditions: that it take place early in pregnancy and be used only in limited cases (rape, incest, and perhaps extreme danger to the woman). A small number, while resisting the accusation that they favor "abortion on demand," would insist that women's right and responsibility to choose must be respected. It is interesting to note that polls indicate that more than three-fourths of Catholic women think abortion is morally acceptable in cases of rape, incest, a severely defective fetus, or when pregnancy threatens the woman's health. In other words, most Catholic women in the United States do not accept the absolutist position.

Moral theologians who question the absolutist stand do so on several grounds. Most important, perhaps, is the question of whether, or at what point, the fertilized ovum or the fetus becomes human or a person with rights. Absolutists tend to see this moment as that of conception itself, while nonabsolutists find serious reasons for doubting that. Looking at the historical record, absolutists find a consistent Christian tradition of horror at abortion from the first generations of the Church. Looking at the same evidence, nonabsolutists find little evidence and indeed argue that until a Vatican decision in the late nineteenth century, abortion was a relatively minor issue about which there was considerable diversity. Finally the type of moral reasoning varies. Absolutists utilize a type of reasoning that proceeds from clear principles to deduce what must be done in practice, whereas nonabsolutists emphasize the need to make moral decisions in context and the unavoidability of ambiguity and competing moral claims that cannot be decisively adjudicated.

A separate but related question is that of the legal status of abortion. If abortion is absolutely evil, it should be outlawed. Some absolutists will not be satisfied until all abortion is outlawed, no matter what the state of public opinion. The more thoughtful, including, one presumes, most bishops, believe that laws must represent some degree of consensus. Cardinal Bernardin, for example, believes that the 1973 Supreme Court decision allowing "abortion on demand" goes beyond the actual consensus of Americans. The prevailing strategy among the bishops has been to lobby for legislation that would restrict abortions and be politically feasible. However, even Catholics who personally agree that abortion is wrong may disagree over the wisdom of enacting legislation.

In practice, the Catholic church has sometimes appeared to be allied with a "single issue" right-to-life constituency. Thus, during the 1984 election campaign, Cardinal John O'Connor and other bishops entered into public controversies with Governor Mario Cuomo of New York and vice-presidential candidate Geraldine Ferraro, not over their stands on abortion but on their positions on abortion legislation. The implication seemed to be that the immorality of abortion was so clear that Catholics should make a candidate's position on abortion legislation the primary criterion for voting decisions. Cardinal Bernardin and the bishops' conference as a whole made statements to the effect that the basis for such decisions should be the whole range of "life issues" (war, poverty, capital punishment, as well as abortion). At the very least, it was clear that the bishops, despite their nominal acceptance of a consistent life ethic, weigh in very differently on public issues.

It is not difficult to see why some—especially women—see the Catholic position on abortion as closely connected to its positions on sexuality and its traditional attitudes toward women. According to official teaching, the only licit sexual activity is that between spouses that does not artificially prevent conception. From such a principle, accepted as "natural law," it logically follows that contraception, pre- or extra-marital sexual activity, and even masturbation are intrinsically wrong or sinful. The prohibition against divorce is similarly based on a conception of marriage as a lifelong unbreakable bond (buttressed by Jesus' sayings against divorce).

In these questions, as well as abortion, the bishops believe they are defending natural law—not divine revelation. That few besides Catholics accept such a "natural law" understanding of sexuality—when in principle it should be clear from human experience and reason—undercuts its credibility. The fact that its most vehement defenders are a celibate hierarchy fuels the suspicion that the Vatican's insistence on sexual morality is closely connected to its own authority. If the Church backtracked on contraception, where could it draw the line? In fact the overwhelming majority of American Catholic women—some 90 percent—do not accept the official teaching on contraception. Polls indicate that most priests agree. Indeed, on this point moral theologians express a certain amount of respectful dissent within the Church. While seeking to maintain something of the natural-law tradition, they argue that Catholic moral theology should pay more attention to sexuality as actually experienced and be less concerned to impose abstract rules.

Strictly speaking, the cases of sexual morality and abortion are not parallel. According to official Catholic teaching, abortion is immoral, not because of its connection to sexuality, but because it is the taking of human life. In practice, however, the issue seems to be closely connected to the questions of sexuality, the role of women, and Church authority. All Catholics would agree that abortion is an evil; what some question, as we have noted above, is the absolutist approach to morality found in official statements.

As is obvious, there is more diversity among Catholics than is recognized in official circles. In 1984 a group called Catholics for a Free Choice published a full-page ad in the *New York Times* titled a "Catholic Statement on Pluralism and Abortion." The ad argued that the Church should acknowledge the existence of a de facto diversity of views on abortion among Catholics. Eighty Catholic theologians had signed on the condition of anonymity, that is, they feared reprisals. A number of respected lay theologians signed. What attracted most attention was the presence of twenty-four sisters, two priests, and two brothers. Vatican response was immediate in the form of pressure on the signers and their religious superiors, essentially threatening to withdraw the congregations' recognition if they did not force the signers to recant. The priests and brothers soon indicated their adherence to official teaching. In most cases some formula was found whereby the sisters could make some statement of loyalty without violating their own consciences and thus remain in their religious congregations. Two sisters on principle refused to sign such a statement; they were not expelled from their congregations, but in the end, they withdrew. Although many U.S. bishops deplored the way the Vatican handled the matter, they did nothing to defend the signers. Sister Maureen Fiedler, one of the signers, later reflected that by choosing not to continue to argue their case publicly and by accepting a face-saving deal with the Vatican, the sisters had once more submitted to patriarchal domination.

The whole process was painful. Those who signed the ad found themselves torn: on the one hand, their Catholicism was a very important part of their identity, and yet their experience as women had led them to question the Church's absolutism on abortion. They were also aware that significant numbers of their fellow Catholics do not accept the absolutist position. Even some Catholics who accepted the official position saw the Vatican action as an ugly abuse of patriarchal Church power. Since this was the period in which the Vatican refused to turn over Archbishop Paul Marcinkus to Italian authorities for his alleged role in banking fraud allegedly totaling billions of dollars, the Vatican's zeal for morality hardly looked like a "seamless garment."

In itself the official position on abortion would seem quite detachable from the bishops' letters on peace and the economy. Since, however, it is the bishops who have stressed the "consistent ethic of life" as an important link, further discussion of Church authority is relevant to the letters.

ROME AND THE LETTERS

As chapters 3 and 5 abundantly illustrate, the bishops buttressed their central arguments with ample quotes from papal documents, especially those of Pope John Paul II. His 1982 statement—not moral reasoning—was the centerpiece of their treatment of deterrence, and his encyclicals, especially *Laborem Exercens*, are often invoked in the economics pastoral.

Yet the very enterprise of the pastoral leaders and the assertion of leadership involved in them is not to the entire satisfaction of some in the Vatican, including the pope. During the pope's 1987 trip through the United States, one would have expected him to make liberal use of both letters. The fact that in a major meeting with all the bishops in southern California he did not even mention the letters, and he virtually ignored them during his dozens of speeches and homilies across the United States, was not an oversight but a message.

That coolness is part of a larger pattern of Vatican reservation over the growing assertiveness of episcopal conferences. For example, Cardinal Joseph Ratzinger, the prefect of the Congregation for the Doctrine of the Faith, whose task is that of overseeing orthodoxy, has said,

> We must not forget that the episcopal conferences have no theological basis, they do not belong to the structure of the

Church, as willed by Christ, that cannot be eliminated; they have only a practical, concrete function.

No episcopal conference, as such, has a teaching mission; its documents have no weight of their own save that of the consent given to them by the individual bishops.

For Ratzinger this position is a matter of

safeguarding the very nature of the Catholic church which is based on an episcopal structure and not on a kind of federation of national churches. The national level is not an ecclesial dimension. It must once again become clear that in each diocese there is only one shepherd and teacher of the faith in communion with the other pastors and teachers and with the Vicar of Christ.

In other words, as Christ set it up, the Church has a "Vicar" in Rome and individual bishops—but not national bishops' conferences. Ratzinger fears that the new role taken by national conferences means that individual bishops are abdicating their authority to bureaucracies. Is he implying, one might ask, that the Vatican bureaucracy—including his own office—was instituted by Christ?

Most Scripture scholars and theologians today do not view the historical models of Church ministry and authority (priests, bishops, pope) as having been directly "instituted" by Jesus. While ministries and Church offices come from the earliest Christian communities, their historical forms have varied extensively. The very model of "bishop" owes a great deal to the situation of cities in the ancient world and to existing Roman and, later on, medieval models of civil authority. The authority system in which individual bishops relate directly to Rome—which Ratzinger seeks to strengthen—owes a great deal to the relationship between feudal lords and their emperor. It is of course buttressed by the theology of recent centuries invoked by Ratzinger as though it were incontestable. To others, however, such a theology seems to be designed primarily to justify papal authority.

In the twenty-five years since the Council, the Vatican has found itself repeatedly trying to curb dissent and stifle currents in the Church seen as unorthodox or dangerous. Some have already been mentioned: controversies over contraception, sexual morality in general, homosexuality, and abortion, and particularly the strong-arm tactics used against the signers of the *New York Times* ad. We may also add the long conflict with Swiss theologian Hans Küng, who questioned papal infallibility among other things and who in 1979 was finally declared to be not a "Catholic" theologian; a campaign against Latin American liberation theology, including interrogation of the Peruvian Gustavo Gutierrez, the silencing for almost a year of the Brazilian Leonardo Boff, and a 1984 document by Ratzinger severely criticizing liberation theology; an adamant refusal to consider the possibility of ordination of women to the priesthood; a policy of appointing conservative bishops to the Dutch Catholic church against majority sentiment there as a way of curbing liberal practices.

Such actions do not come from the Vatican alone but form part of a larger movement of backlash against directions taken by many Catholics after Vatican II. In the early 1970s a movement called Communion and Liberation was formed with the express intention of combatting such tendencies. Although it is scarcely known in the United States, it is a growing force in some countries. Around the same time, a theological journal called *Communio* was set up expressly to counter a multilanguage review called *Concilium*, which was a medium of exchange for post–Vatican II theology.

Under Pope John Paul II such developments have been encouraged. The backlash has taken programmatic form with Ratzinger's rise to head the Congregation for the Doctrine of the Faith. It is sometimes encapsulated in the word *restoration*: Ratzinger's aim, shared by the pope, is to "restore" to the Church a sense of doctrinal security that is in danger of evaporating under the impact of the postconciliar winds.

Two American cases, those of Father Charles Curran and of Archbishop Raymond Hunthausen, illustrate this. Curran would be rated a moderate among American Catholic moral theologians today. His Vatican file began in the 1960s, when he was among those who expressed respectful dissent on contraception and was defended by students and faculty at Catholic University on the grounds of academic freedom. In 1979 the Vatican reactivated its accusations against him and began a long process that eventually led to pressures on the university to fire him. Efforts were made at a compromise solution whereby Curran would continue at Catholic University, but when Church authorities insisted that he not teach theology, he sued in civil court for breach of contract. For the Vatican the Curran case had an exemplary effect: it was asserting its right to exercise vigilance over Catholic teaching. Teachers and administrators of Catholic universities, for that same reason, saw it as a threat to academic freedom.

While Bishop Matthew Clark of Rochester, Curran's own bishop, expressed respect for him as a priest and as a competent theologian and voiced a fear that action against him could harm Catholic theology, he did not directly criticize the Vatican action. None of the other bishops publicly defended Curran's rights as a theologian. This is strange in view of the fact that he was one of the very few theologians invited as an expert witness before the drafting committees of both pastoral letters. No doubt many of the bishops share the Vatican's criticisms of Curran, but it stretches credulity to believe that all do. That none publicly dared express solidarity with him eloquently testifies to the power of the Vatican system.

For the bishops, an even more painful case was that of their colleague, Raymond Hunthausen, the archbishop of Seattle. In a rather public way the Vatican ordered an investigation of Hunthausen with regard to several pastoral practices in his archdiocese (e.g., liturgy, pastoral practice in the area of sexuality). At one point its "solution" was to appoint Bishop Donald Wuerl as an auxiliary bishop to Hunthausen: formally he would remain archbishop, but Wuerl was given authority over major areas of decision. It was a highly unusual and humiliating gesture, all the more striking insofar as the alleged erroneous practices are common in many parts of the U.S. Catholic church. Many suspected that the campaign against Hunthausen had been instigated by conservatives in his military-dependent area (dominated by Boeing), who were outraged at his outspoken advocacy of peace (e.g., he once called the Trident submarine the "Auschwitz of Puget Sound" and personally refused to pay income taxes for war purposes). There was a great outpouring of support for Hunthausen in Seattle and around the country.

At the same November 1986 meeting at which they approved the final text of *Economic Justice for All*, the bishops had to deal with the "Hunthausen affair." Their tack was essentially to support their brother archbishop and express pain over the matter while accepting in principle Rome's right to intervene. Bishop James Malone, speaking for the bishops as a body, said that the conference "has no authority to intervene in the internal affairs of a diocese or in the unique relationship between the pope and individual bishops." While accepting the legitimacy of Rome's actions, he spoke of "misunderstandings" and likened the whole matter to "pain" within a family. After a decent interval, the conservative Bishop Wuerl was transferred, Hunthausen's authority was reinstated, and he was given an auxiliary bishop more congenial to him.

From the Vatican's viewpoint, the Curran and Hunthausen cases were linked insofar as they represented the danger of an American Catholicism that needed curbing. As a group the U.S. bishops defended their brother bishop as far as they thought they could. Curran, however, received no support from the bishops. At their November 1987 meeting, after he was already gone from Catholic University, they issued a statement on the relationship between theologians and the Church's teaching authority, seeking to clarify mutual roles.

Some might wonder why the bishops without exception accept official doctrine and authority. Eugene Kennedy, summarizing a psychological study by psychologist Frank Kobler, gives some clues. The bishops "quite effectively build their existences around the ecclesiastical institution, identifying their 'calling' with their heavily administrative obligations." The fact that they are conservative theologically and liberal socially both stands in continuity with earlier generations of U.S. bishops and in line with church social teaching. "The bishops are not and never will be rebels against the pope or Church authority. They may explore the full limits of their newly emphasized collegiality, but they perceive this as authority and responsibility that comes to them from the Church itself and hence in harmony with their dedication." The bishops are "extremely bright" but with a few exceptions they are not "intellectuals interested in the world of ideas." They are convinced that their office comes to them from Jesus Christ and they are especially loyal to the pope.

On a less exalted note, it is quite clear that any priest who expresses dissent on issues considered critical automatically disqualifies himself from consideration for the episcopacy. Vatican officials in fact scrutinize the record of potential bishops in order to assure themselves of their loyalty, especially on issues such as contraception, the ordination of women, and abortion. Thus, the reasons for episcopal acquiescence to Rome are not mysterious.

Another incident in late 1987 seemed to weaken bishops' conferences. The board of the bishops' conference issued guidelines on AIDS education in Catholic schools and institutions. The statement showed compassion for AIDS victims and avoided moralizing. While upholding traditional Catholic teaching on sexual morality, the bishops nevertheless said that condoms could be mentioned in AIDS education. Cardinals Bernard Law of Boston, John O'Connor of New York, and some others publicly expressed disagreement. Their understanding of a "consistent life ethic" obviously meant placing a higher value on avoiding the sin of contraception in a sexual act already regarded as sinful (outside wedlock) than on halting the spread of a killer disease. It is extremely rare for bishops to air their disagreements in public. The fact that Law is considered to represent the point of view of Ratzinger and Pope John Paul II led some to see this action as clearly intended to weaken the U.S. bishops' conference.

The Vatican attack escalated in February 1988 with a draft of a statement on the "Theological and Juridical Status of Episcopal Conferences." This document codifies the objections raised by Ratzinger. The Vatican seeks to deprive national conferences of authority and justifies its action on the grounds that it is thereby protecting individual bishops. The net result is not likely to be greater freedom for individual bishops but greater subjection to the Vatican, as the Hunthausen affair shows quite clearly. One priest paraphrased Ben Franklin saying that if the bishops "don't hang together, the Vatican can hang them separately whenever and for whatever it likes."

These controversies are clearly part of the context in which the pastoral letters on nuclear weapons and the economy were prepared. Cardinal Ratzinger's reservations about bishops' conferences, although expressed in theological terms, reflect a fear that a growing role for bishops' conferences must mean a diminished role for the papacy. With such a zero-sum idea of authority, Ratzinger does not seem to see the other possibility: that an obsessional assertion of authority in defiance of the experience of many Catholics in fact undermines the very authority being asserted.

To turn the point around: it seems quite clear that the process employed by the U.S. bishops gave their letters a hearing they would not have received had they simply been issued in a top-down fashion. There is no inherent reason to believe that the papacy's real authority would be jeopardized by a more collegial style of governance, although that would curtail its absolutist governing style. One may suspect that Catholicism will be strengthened, not weakened, to the extent that it advances further along the road of consultation and participation followed in *The Challenge of Peace* and *Economic Justice for All*.

· 7 ·

FURTHER QUESTIONS

N either *The Challenge of Peace* nor *Economic Justice for All* is a ringing manifesto; both are subtle documents of consensus whose more immediate policy proposals (full employment policies, changes in welfare procedures, safeguarding the family farm, Third World debt relief) fit within the bounds of political discourse in the United States, albeit on the left-liberal side. At their more visionary moments the bishops propose

- A fundamental shift away from military spending toward meeting human needs

- A new kind of relationship between the United States and the Soviet Union

- A "new American experiment" to extend the principles of democracy into economic enterprises and economic life

· The creation of a supranational political authority that could regulate interstate conflicts, prevent war, and deal with economic, political, and environmental problems of a worldwide scope for the common good of humankind.

The bishops do not present such proposals as ideals for some future age when the world is ready. On the contrary, they are convinced that today's world already demands rapid and immediate progress in these directions. Present institutions and attitudes, such as the absolute status of the nation-state, are blocking the resolution of our accumulated problems.

In this closing chapter I would like to offer some further thoughts not so much on the texts of the pastoral letters but rather on possible further implications both for the Church and for U.S. society.

A THEOLOGY OF PEACEMAKING

More than once the bishops call for the development of an interdisciplinary theology of peace, drawing on "biblical studies, systematic and moral theology, ecclesiology, and the experience and insights of members of the Church who have struggled in various ways to make and keep the peace." Such a theology

should ground the task of peacemaking solidly in the biblical vision of the kingdom of God, then place it centrally in the ministry of the Church. It should specify the obstacles in the way of peace, as these are understood theologically and in the social and political sciences. (CP, 25)

In addition, this theology should clarify the contribution of the Church to peacemaking and how it relates to other groups and to institutions in society, and it must include a "message of hope." Elsewhere they note that the principles of nonviolent action should be "part of any Christian theology of peace" (226). To theologians they express their belief that "we have only begun the journey toward a theology of peace; without your specific contributions this desperately needed dimension of our faith will not be realized. Through your help we may provide new vision and wisdom for church and state" (304).

Curiously, although Archbishop Weakland has been more involved with theology and teaching than Cardinal Bernardin, the economic pastoral does not make any similar direct appeals to theologians but rather urges further reflection on Catholic social teaching for research into many specific areas of policy. The difference, however, may be one of terminology.

The Church, of course, does not operate on theology—any more than governments operate on political science. At its best, theology is a reflection on the experience of individual believers, congregations, and the whole Church in their efforts to live out their faith. Theologians have played an important role in the evolution of modern Catholicism. For example, Vatican II codified several decades of theological work. Hence, the call to theologians and scholars in the letters is not surprising.

What is somewhat surprising is the bishops' attitude that a theology of peace is only beginning, since there is a steady output of theological articles and books on questions of peace and justice. It seems unlikely that what they envision is simply more publications. I would suggest that their intuition is rather that peace and justice should not only be separate topics in theology—a subdivision of ethics—but that they should become more central to the theological enterprise as a whole. Thus, to take only one example, in a Christology course, a professor and class might develop the implications of the passages on Jesus in both pastorals. That is, they could reread the Gospels and examine the various Christologies throughout history with an eye to peacemaking and the witness of poverty. Similarly, they could ask what the Lordship of Jesus means in a world divided into hostile camps, or what the eucharist meal means when people cannot produce or obtain enough food.

It is my impression that professional Catholic theologians have yet to give the pastoral letters the importance they deserve. Understandably, much of their attention is absorbed by the kinds of questions discussed in the previous chapter and their own freedom as scholars in the Church. Nevertheless, in coming years, I hope to see theologians and other Catholic intellectuals do much more to respond to the invitation contained in the pastoral letters.

Although the term normally conjures up an academic image, theology should be seen in broader terms. There is a theology at work in the everyday life of parishes: in worship services and even in the way parish staffs budget their time. Pastoral options involve trade-offs, and choices made reflect theological positions. How should work with sick people be evaluated in comparison with working in coalitions on community problems? The fact that the theology underlying such choices made may be unreflective does not make it less operative.

However, it is perhaps important from time to time to reflect consciously on that operative theology. Suppose for example, the people of a parish were to use the pastoral letters, not simply in order to learn what the bishops have to say about public issues, but in order to examine their own activity in the context of their neighborhood and wider environs.

Taking off from the letters, priests, sisters, and laypeople might formulate and seek to answer questions like the following: What is the economic basis of this region? Who are the largest employers? What is the unemployment level? Is joblessness increasing or decreasing? Do the jobs being generated have a future or are they dead-end jobs? What proportion of local jobs are in military-related industries? What human impacts do we observe in this parish and in our city or region? What do we observe in the lives of women and men and families? Do we observe important things that the bishops failed to see or passed over very lightly?

Such inquiry might lead to a second kind of question: What kind of service does our parish render to the larger community? Are we—or should we be—involved in aiding the homeless? Besides providing services to individuals and families, should we as a parish explore the possibility of engaging in advocacy on behalf of the poor? What steps can we take to put into practice the suggestions of the bishops? Should we modify our worship services to make them more clearly moments of dedication to peace and to community service? Should we pray explicitly for our "enemies" in the Soviet Union and elsewhere? Can we take steps to become more peaceful ourselves?

The intuition here is that both letters not only contain valuable elements for the presence of the institutional Church in areas of public policy (for example, congressional testimony on specific legislation by the bishops) and for the personal life of individual Catholics (business people making decisions) but also that they should become part of the "operational theology" of parishes and other pastoral institutions.

WOMEN'S VOICE

On each drafting team, bishops, staff, and consultants, there was only one woman; only two women gave formal testimony on the peace pastoral, and perhaps a tenth of those testifying on the economics pastoral were women. In the bishops' defense it could be said that the representation of women in similar endeavors in government or the corporate world might not be very different. They cannot change the way the Catholic church operates; the Vatican not only stoutly resists any consideration of ordination of women to the priesthood, let alone the episcopacy, but it apparently regards the maleness of the clergy as a doctrinal, not a merely disciplinary, matter. Official Church teaching continues to see women and men as equal but different. To many women this rationale parallels that given for apartheid; the practice of the Church has all the marks of plain sexism.

Given the nature of Vatican authority, the bishops could only strive to be sensitive to the experience and concerns of women. However, as one sister told me in the corridors around the bishops' November 1987 meeting, "It's not enough just to have women's input. Decision making should be male and female." Ultimately this is a matter of justice. The Church undercuts its own demands for justice when it excludes women. In the longer run, the answer would seem to be the admission of women to all ranks of Church ministry and leadership. By hindsight, their exclusion will probably look more like a shibboleth than a matter of Christian doctrine. The all-male ministry will someday go the way of the Latin mass. In the meantime, justice would seem to demand that the Church move toward equality in decision making.

This impasse is illustrated by the U.S. bishops' efforts to draw up a pastoral letter on women in the Church and society. A first draft was published in April 1988. To a degree that was quite innovative in Catholicism, the bishops listened to women. Although the committee itself was made up of five bishops, all the consultants and staff were women. Reflecting the operating style of many women's organizations, each major section of the document first expressed women's experience (voices of affirmation and voices of alienation), then moved to Catholic teaching (reflecting on our heritage), before making some pastoral observations. The influence of feminist scriptural scholarship and theology was quite evident (for example, the reminder that the first messengers of Jesus' resurrection were women). Sexism was denounced as "sinful," and there were many good statements about violence against women. Even on the question of the ordination of women, the bishops listened and reflected; however, they reaffirmed the Vatican's 1976 "normative" ruling on the question, encourage "further study . . . to deepen our understanding," and urged that women be enabled to serve in lesser ministries. Reactions among Catholic women varied from the most traditionalist, who saw it as representing a vocal minority, to many women who are striving to be both Catholics and feminists, to some who saw it as quite insufficient.

Without a doubt *The Challenge of Peace* and *Economic Justice for All* would have been stronger and would have spoken more penetratingly to Catholics and the general public had women been thoroughly a part of the drafting and decision-making process. The all-male nature of the hierarchy and clergy impoverishes the Catholic church's understanding of the gospel it preaches and constricts its ability to communicate its message.

ECOLOGICAL REVERENCE

Apart from the section of the economics pastoral on farm policy and the peace pastoral's awareness that nuclear weapons threaten the "entire planet," there is little ecological perspective in either letter. One person close to the drafting process of the economics letter told me that the bishops were loath to venture into an area where study was thus far inconclusive. For example, many now see the "limits-to-growth" projections of the early 1970s to have been too alarmist.

However, certain general trends seem clear enough. For example, despite the oil "glut" of the 1980s, world petroleum resources are finite, and scarcity may return even in the 1990s. It is inconceivable that there is enough petroleum in the world to permit Third World countries to develop a way of life based on private automobiles. It is quite possible that children already born in the United States will live to see the day when our own use of oil will seem profligate. Something similar may be true of the industrial and military use of certain metals.

Present economic and political systems, however, are not only incapable of taking into account future generations; they seem unable to respond even to present ecological damage. For Canadians it is obvious that acid rain from U.S. industries are destroying their forests, but the Reagan administration has refused to do more than fund further study. Conventional economics sees environmental costs as "externalities"; they are real enough but they are passed off to society and future generations. Electoral horizons tend to prevent elected officials from taking the long-range view required by environmental seriousness.

It would seem especially appropriate for the Church to cultivate ecological reverence. If one of the sources of the Western hubris about our rightful dominion over nature is the traditional reading of the Genesis command to "Subdue the earth," it is incumbent on the Church to search its own tradition for a more adequate understanding of how humankind is embedded in the web of life on the planet. While the bishops were suitably modest in noting that Catholic social teaching on the environment and natural resources is "still in the process of development," by making the topic so marginal they passed up an opportunity to contribute to that development. What is called for is not only an awareness of many of the current and emerging ecological crises: pollution of water and air, depletion of tropical rain forests, the "greenhouse effect," advancing desertification, sinking water tables, and so forth, but a spirituality that can develop a religious awe and respect for the earth—which ultimately would deepen a sense of God's presence.

Undertaking any more pastoral letters of the scope of those on peace, the economy, and women would seem questionable, since it would inevitably dilute their effect. Nevertheless, if there is a general topic that cries out for a similar development, it is that of a religious and ethical understanding of ecology.

THE CHURCH IN HISTORY

Neither document pays much attention to history. Perhaps the drafters felt that any historical passages that went beyond a sketch would make the documents far longer and would entail further controversy. One exception in the documents themselves is a relatively detailed history of legislation favoring land ownership (EJA, 219ff.) In any case, the perspectives provided in the letters demand a deepened sense of history.

With regard to the Church, it is clear that much remains to be done to make Catholics aware of their own tradition of peace-making and work for justice. To take an obvious example, the "option for the poor" should shed light on the meaning of Saint Francis of Assisi for today. Again, it would be useful for Catholics in the pews to have a better understanding of the history of American Catholicism. On the one hand, it would be helpful to recall the alliance between the Church and organized labor more than a half century ago and on the other to reflect on the reasons for the long delay in raising moral questions about nuclear policy.

The bishops propose a new American experiment in the economy similar to that initiated by the founders in American political institutions. Read unreflectively, their document could reinforce the celebratory versions of U.S. history that ignore the fact that originally only propertied white males participated in that experiment. To take a more critical view is not to disparage the greatness of that experiment but to give due credit to the many ordinary citizens who have struggled to make institutions measure up to the original promise.

END OF "THE AMERICAN CENTURY"

Americans today have grown up taking it for granted that the United States is and should be number one. Throughout this century and especially after 1945, the United States has enjoyed predominance, perhaps best symbolized by the role of the dollar in the international economy. To one degree or another most Americans believe the United States embodies a superior morality in the world. The pastoral letters do little to challenge such feelings and in some ways seem to reinforce them. They seem to assume that the United States will remain predominant in the world economy and that U.S. actions on the world stage are at least motivated by high purposes.

However, there is good reason to believe that the "American century" is over—that it lasted from 1945 to 1970. Since then, for example, the wages of American workers in real terms have not grown. U.S. industry has lost its competitive edge over the resurgent economies of Western Europe and Japan and faces increasing competition from Third World countries. Much of the political debate of the last two decades may be seen as an effort to deal with the consequences of this relative decline. Ronald Reagan has shamelessly but effectively exploited the doubts and insecurities of ordinary Americans by appealing to the myth of the United States as number one. Rather than restoring American preeminence, however, his administration seems to have delayed the day of reckoning.

Suppose it is impossible for the United States to return to its former economic power. Suppose investment advisor Michael Moffit is correct when he says that the United States "has entered a period of economic and industrial decline that is likely to be permanent, much like the decline in British industrial supremacy that began around 1880." In Moffit's view, this is not the result of any particular policy but of the globalization of the economy through transnational corporations. He foresees "a nasty decline in the standard of living in the United States." Not surprisingly, politicians are not eager to admit such a possibility.

The bishops wisely shied away from attempting to predict the future, and there is no need for them to embrace all the details of an analysis like Moffit's. However, might it not be proper for the Church to question the myth that America must be number one? There is a spiritual dimension to this question. Our identity and self-image is to some extent tied up with this notion. Many of us would feel diminished if we had to recognize that the United States is simply one nation among others. Possessing nuclear weapons covertly reinforces our sense of being number one. Is it possible that having the ultimate weapon makes the U.S. inability to force the Nicaraguan government to cry uncle all the more frustrating?

This is difficult terrain. One of the stock arguments of Catholic neoconservatives is that the "religious left" absorbed a "hate America" and "blame America" mentality from the 1960s. What I am suggesting here is simply that we must seriously consider whether American economic predominance may not be irretrievable and whether there are not cultural and spiritual consequences that should be faced squarely.

CHURCH AND DÉTENTE

Anti-Sovietism is the shadow side of the assumption that America must be number one, especially in moral purpose. The Soviet Union's evil and its multiple failures highlight essential American goodness. The Catholic church played a major role in reinforcing post–World War II Cold War ideology. One need only point to the high visibility of Cardinal Spellman of New York. In their letter the bishops suggest that the superpowers can and must come to a new kind of relationship, but their proposal is hedged by so much criticism of the USSR that the prophetic element is muffled.

What is called for is engagement with the real Soviet Union, with its history, its way of life, its culture. There is no need to demonize the Soviet system: virtually no American would choose to live under such a system, and its many crimes are a matter of historical record. However, the Russians and the other peoples of the USSR can only move toward reform by appropriating that history, not by leaping out of it; they can shape a more workable and more just economy only by starting with their present economy.

The advent of Mikhail Gorbachev to leadership of the USSR was not a chance occurrence; he and his government represent the advent of people whose careers have developed during the post-Stalin period. The proposed reforms, both economic and political, are not the brainchild of an individual but represent the pent-up demands of a generation. There is a growing sense, especially in Europe that this new period of détente may signal the end of the forty-year-old Cold War. The "new moment" that the bishops saw in 1983, largely as a result of public alarm over the accelerating arms race, begins to have a more positive content.

I would suggest that this situation calls for initiatives within the Catholic church. To take a very simple one, should not prayer for the Soviet Union, its people and its leaders, be a regular feature of Catholic worship in the United States? The fact that for years at the peace-minded parish I attend the congregation has prayed for literally a dozen trouble spots every Sunday: countries in Central America, the Middle East, Africa—but never for the Soviet Union—indicated a blind spot to me. I would further urge that there be increased contact between U.S. Catholics and the Soviet Union: church-to-church contacts, both in the United States and in the USSR, delegations of Americans in the USSR and of Russians in our country. At some point some small groups could spend extended periods of time in the USSR. One possibility might be for theologians to spend time studying in church settings in the Soviet Union. Could Catholic schools and universities give particular emphasis to the Russian language and to the study of the USSR and the eastern bloc?

The aim of these and many other such possibilities would not be to soften U.S. resolve but rather to search for ways to obey the biblical injunction to love one's enemy, as well as concrete ways to make it possible for both present superpowers to find a common *modus vivendi.*

THE DEADLY CONNECTION

Although in shorthand form *The Challenge of Peace* is called the "peace pastoral," its central focus is nuclear weapons. The bishops draw some further connections, especially the scandal of an increasing military budget and growing arms sales when human needs cry out for satisfaction. Nevertheless, much more could be done to develop what has been called the "deadly connection" between nuclear weapons and an overall military mind-set and approach to the world. It is especially striking that the bishops, who have repeatedly opposed the Reagan administration's Central America policy, did not devote at least some attention to interventionary war. For Latin Americans, including the elites, it is clear that the underlying reason for U.S. intervention in Central America is not communism but "Monroeism": the unilaterally declared U.S. right to intervene in the region. U.S. liberals and conservatives share an (often unconscious) assumption that U.S. hegemony is a natural state of affairs. For Latin Americans, however, the issue is self-determination.

More broadly, in the 1980s much of U.S. policy toward the Third World has come to be seen under the umbrella concept of "low-intensity conflict," which subsumes economic aid and diplomacy. To have critiqued the underlying assumptions of such an approach to the world may not have been feasible for the bishops, many of whom seem to share the ideology of Cold War liberalism. However, that may emerge as one of the ways in which the insights of the pastoral letters may be further extended.

Economic Justice for All seems to avoid focusing directly on the giant corporation. The bishops stake out a middle ground, rejecting both "unfettered free enterprise" and "statist solutions." They enthusiastically favor a broad extension of productive property, most concretely in their bias in favor of the family farm. They have words of praise for entrepreneurs and business people.

The bishops do raise questions about the impact of mergers and hostile takeovers on local communities. They state their belief that return on investment alone is not "an adequate rationale for shareholder decisions." Noting that the whole question is complex, they call for "serious, long-term research and experimentation in this area" (305–306).

One has the impression that the bishops wanted to avoid directly considering the question of large corporations. To do so might have opened them up even more to accusations of expressing radical-leftist positions. As a result, however, their blessing over small human-scale entrepreneurship tends to pass by osmosis to the corporate capitalist economy as a whole. They might have spelled out more directly the increasing concentration of the U.S. economy in the hands of the largest corporations, just as they noted concentration of wealth, income, and land ownership. That is, they could have examined the structure of the economy and especially the power wielded by giant corporations.

Is the "principle of subsidiarity" (see pages 90–91) relevant to corporate capitalism? In defending the family farm, the bishops invoke extra-economic considerations, especially the value of a way of life for farm families and rural communities. To this argument they add the assertion that family farms are able to take advantage of economies of scale. Something of a similar nature is argued in connection with plant closings, namely, that such decisions should not be made without taking into account the rights of workers and of local communities. Moreover, the notion that the principles of democracy should be extended to firms points in a similar direction. This is not rhetorical corporation bashing; I am simply suggesting that the principles enunciated in the letters point toward a more clear-sighted examination of the structure of corporate capitalism and the increasing concentration of the largest corporations. To examine is not to condemn. Moreover, even managers of state socialist economies want to do business with transnational corporations. However, corporations need not be considered untouchable if the economy itself is a human product and subject to modification by conscious human action.

AFFINITIES WITH ANARCHISM?

Might it be profitable to explore and develop the affinities between Catholic social teaching and anarchist thought? The notion may seem puzzling, since Catholicism seems to be a total system. Indeed, some suspect that Catholics or ex-Catholics are attracted to Marxism precisely because it seems to promise a total answer: like Christopher Durang's Sister Mary Ignatius, Karl Marx "explains it all." To the extent that the bishops raised questions about the present economy, they were assumed to be crypto-socialist.

Here, however, I have been suggesting that implicit in the bishops' use of Catholic social teaching may be an affinity with the "communitarianism" of some philosophers. One prominent strain of anarchist thinking stresses the need to live in a human-scale community, in connection with a local ecology and in a history, language, and tradition. Both capitalism and socialism are criticized not only for their top-down nature, but because their institutions—the corporation or the state—are largely beyond the direct experience of most citizens. The ideal is for human life— in production, politics, and culture—to take place at the local level on a human scale. The basic political unit should be the local body of citizens. Is not the "principle of subsidiarity" somewhat anarchist? It is perhaps not accidental that E. F. Schumacher was Catholic, as is Ivan Illich. There is a clear strain of anarchism in the Catholic Worker movement, as well as in many Catholic peace activists (for example, Daniel and Philip Berrigan and Elizabeth McAlister).

A recent development of anarchism is bioregionalism. The root idea of this movement is that we humans do in fact live in discernible regions, each with its own characteristics. We should live in harmony within these regions rather than do violence to them and to the earth. For example, bioregionalists believe we should consume locally produced food rather than trucking it across the continent or flying or shipping it from another hemisphere. Human ingenuity should be turned to developing available resources to the utmost while remaining in harmony with the local ecology. Should the principles of *Economic Justice for All* lead to further exploration of bioregionalism?

Of course this affinity to anarchism, if it exists, sits alongside other elements in the Catholic tradition, especially bishops' (and popes') plea for a supranational political entity similar to that made by "world order" thinkers. Catholicism seems to resist the characteristically modern assumption that one's loyalties are almost exclusively to the nation-state. Drawing on its own historical experience, Catholicism urges a loyalty to one's local community and to the world community as well.

EXTENDING PARTICIPATION

The bishops at one point say, "As we have proposed a new experiment in collaboration and participation in decision making by all those affected at all levels of U.S. society, so we also commit the Church to become a model of collaboration and participation" (358). Taken seriously this would seem to commit the Church to its own self-democratization. The wording is general and does not translate into a one-person-one-vote model. Indeed, the tenor of what the bishops say about participation in firms seems to lean more toward a consensus model.

The bishops' enthusiasm for participation in society does not shine through the everyday workings of the Catholic church.

Although participatory mechanisms, ranging from the parish council to the synod of bishops, have been introduced since Vatican II, all such mechanisms are for consultation, not decision making.

Many see a sharp contrast between the open process followed in the pastoral letters on peace and on the economy, and the inability or the refusal to take lay experience into account with regard to the role of women and questions related to sexuality. From the official viewpoint, these matters are closed and hence such consultation is out of the question. There is little likelihood of significant change during the present papacy. Nevertheless, it is possible to imagine that at some future point the Church will experiment with "collaboration and participation" in areas that are currently out of bounds.

There are, clearly, any number of loose ends here. It seems only fitting, since the bishops' letters themselves conclude with a strong sense that they are in no way settling the questions they raise, but providing a stimulus for reflection and action.

The U.S. Catholic bishops' primary purpose in writing the letters is not to throw their weight behind particular public policy questions. Rather they want to give an example of how to approach major issues facing our society from an ethical viewpoint, and to exemplify what the Catholic tradition might contribute. Their aim is not to tell others what to think or how to vote, but to show what kinds of criteria should be taken into account. They have provided no detailed blueprint, but they do invoke a vision.

I believe—or at least hope—that the 1990s will be a decade of renewed questioning, experimentation, and reform in the United States. Although they were fashioned during the years of ascendant Reaganism, *The Challenge of Peace* and *Economic Justice for All* provide important resources for that renewal.

REFERENCES

Texts of bishops' letters: *The Challenge of Peace: God's Promise and Our Response* (Washington, D.C.: United States Catholic Conference, 1983) and *Economic Justice for All: Pastoral Letter on Catholic Social Teaching and the U.S. Economy* (Washington, D.C.: United States Catholic Conference, 1986). The bishops' conference itself has published each letter in more than one format, and they have been reprinted in several collections of essays. Here all references will be to paragraph numbers, and in many instances the particular letter is indicated by initials: CP for *The Challenge of Peace*, EJA for *Economic Justice for All*. There are several collections of essays commenting on each letter. On the peace pastoral: Philip J. Murnion, ed., *Catholics and Nuclear War: A Commentary on "The Challenge of Peace"—The U.S. Catholic Bishops' Pastoral Letter on War and Peace* (New York: Crossroad, 1983); John T. Pawlikowski, O.S.M., and Donald Senior, C.P., eds., *Biblical and Theological Reflections on "The*

Challenge of Peace" (Wilmington, Del.: Michael Glazier, 1984); William V. O'Brien and John Langan, S.J., eds., The Nuclear Dilemma and the Just War Tradition (Lexington, Mass.: Lexington Books, 1986); Charles J. Reid, Jr., ed., Peace in a Nuclear Age: The Bishops' Pastoral Letter in Perspective (Washington, D.C.: Catholic University of America Press, 1986). On the economics pastoral: John W. Houck and Oliver F. Williams, eds., Catholic Social Teaching and the United States Economy: Working Papers for a Bishops' Pastoral (Washington, D.C.: University Press of America, 1984); R. Bruce Douglass, ed., The Deeper Meaning of Economic Life: Critical Essays on the U.S. Catholic Bishops' Pastoral Letter on the Economy (Washington, D.C.: Georgetown University Press, 1986); and Thomas M. Gannon, S.J., ed., The Catholic Challenge to the American Economy: Reflections on the U.S. Bishops' Pastoral Letter on Catholic Social Teaching and the U.S. Economy, (New York: Macmillan Publishing Co., 1987). Debates on both letters were summarized in the quarterly Theological Studies from 1982 to 1986 in the review articles "Notes on Moral Theology," as well as in several articles. There were also symposia in Commonweal on the peace pastoral (August 13, 1982) and in America on the economics pastoral (May 4, 1985). I have also utilized nine addresses by Cardinal Bernardin on The Challenge of Peace and seventeen by Archbishop Weakland on Economic Justice for All.

INTRODUCTION

Cycles of activism: Arthur Schlesinger, Jr., The Cycles of American History (Boston: Houghton Mifflin Co., 1986), quote from p. 47.

Reactions to letters: George Kennan, New York Times op-ed, May 1, 1983, reprinted in Kenneth Aman, ed., Border Regions of Faith: An Anthology of Religion and Social Change (Maryknoll, N.Y.: Orbis Books, 1987); Tobin and Klein gave testimony to the House Subcommittee on Economic Stabilization on March 19, 1985, reprinted as Lawrence Klein, "Reducing Unemployment

Without Inflation," and James Tobin, "Unemployment, Poverty and Economic Policy," both in *America*, May 4, 1985; remarks of Buckley and Will taken from David S. Broder, "Reagan Conservatives Resent Bishops' 'Untimely' Criticism," *Miami Herald*, op-ed, November 21, 1984, and editorial in *Commonweal*, November 30, 1984 ($100,000 figure also from that editorial); Lehman editorial and Clark letter, Jim Castelli, *The Bishops and the Bomb: Waging Peace in a Nuclear Age* (Garden City, N.Y.: Image Books, 1984), pp. 118ff.; Milton Friedman, "Good Ends, Bad Means," in Thomas Gannon, ed., *The Catholic Challenge to the American Economy* (New York: Macmillan Publishing Co., 1987), p. 99; Alexander Cockburn and Robert Pollin, "Hardheads and Bishops: How to Talk About Economic Strategy," *The Nation* 244, no. 8, February 28, 1987.

Twenty-two percent jump in Catholic nuclear opposition: Andrew Greeley, *American Catholics Since the Council: An Unauthorized Report* (Chicago: Thomas More Press, 1985), pp. 93ff.

CHAPTER 1—A VISION: CATHOLIC AND AMERICAN

Economic and educational rise of Catholics: Andrew M. Greeley, *American Catholics Since the Council: An Unauthorized Report* (Chicago: Thomas More Press, 1985), pp. 25–34; quotes from pp. 27 and 28.

On the bishops: Eugene Kennedy, *Re-Imagining American Catholicism: The American Bishops and Their Pastoral Letters*, (New York: Vintage Books, 1985), chap. 2, "American Bishops: Institutional Men." Study on their educational background and quote is from Thomas J. Reese, S.J., "A Survey of the American Bishops," *America*, November 12, 1983, cited by Kennedy on pp. 44–45. Quotes, Kennedy, pp. 48 and 49.

Process of writing peace pastoral: In *The Bishops and the Bomb*, Castelli provides a detailed account of the drafting and revision process.

Murnion criticism: William E. Murnion, "The Role and Language of the Church in Relation to Public Policy," in Philip J. Murnion, *Catholics and Nuclear War*, pp. 57–70. See also William E. Murnion, "The American Catholic Bishops' Peace Pastoral: A Critique of Its Logic," *Horizons* 13, no. 1 (1986): 67–89.

"Catholic Social Teaching": classic statements in William J. Gibbons, ed., *Seven Great Encyclicals* (New York: Paulist Press, 1963); post–Vatican II statements can be found in Joseph Gremillion, *The Gospel of Peace and Justice: Catholic Social Teaching Since Pope John* (Maryknoll, N.Y.: Orbis Books, 1976); other collections listed in the "Select Bibliography" of *Economic Justice for All* (or in some versions, chap. II, fn. 17). Three divergent treatments: Donal Dorr, *Option for the Poor: A Hundred Years of Vatican Social Teaching* (Maryknoll, N.Y.: Orbis Books, 1983); Michael Novak, *Freedom With Justice: Catholic Social Thought and Liberal Institutions* (San Francisco: Harper & Row, 1984); Gregory Baum, *The Priority of Labor: A Commentary on "Laborem Exercens"* (New York: Paulist Press, 1982). In articles in the *National Catholic Reporter* and in *Daedalus* 111, no. 1 (Winter 1982), Peter Hebblethwaithe has drawn attention to the contrast between Paul VI and John Paul II on the social teaching.

Friedman quote: "Good Ends, Bad Means," in Gannon, *The Catholic Challenge*, p. 105.

Habits discussion: Robert N. Bellah, Richard Madsen, William M. Sullivan, Ann Swidler, Steven M. Tipton, *Habits of the Heart: Individualism and Commitment in American Life* (Berkeley: University of California Press, 1985); see also the collection of readings edited by the same authors, *Individualism and Commitment in American Life: Readings on the Themes of "Habits of the Heart"* (New York: Harper & Row, 1987). Bellah spoke at a major symposium on the economics pastoral at Loyola Marymount University in Los Angeles in July 1987 and wrote on it in "Resurrecting the Common Good," *Commonweal*, December 18, 1987.

CHAPTER 2—SAYING NO TO NUCLEAR WAR

Paul Brians's study: *Nuclear Holocausts: Atomic War in Fiction—1895–1984* (Kent: Ohio State University Press, 1987). Brians lists approximately eight hundred short stories and novels in an appendix.

Background to *The Challenge of Peace*: Robert Scheer, *With Enough Shovels: Reagan, Bush and Nuclear War* (New York: Random House, 1982); "Thinking the Unthinkable: Rising Fears About Nuclear War," *Time* (cover story) March 29, 1982; Peter Steinfels, "The Foreign Policy Context of the Nuclear Debate," in Murnion, *Catholics and Nuclear War*, pp. 330ff. On weapons systems and concepts: Sheila Tobias, Peter Goudinoff, Stefan Leader, and Shelah Leader, *What Kinds of Guns Are They Buying for Your Butter? A Beginner's Guide to Defense, Weaponry, and Military Spending* (New York: William Morrow & Co., 1982). A wide-ranging collection is Len Ackland and Steven Mcguire, eds., *Assessing the Nuclear Age: Selections from the Bulletin of the Atomic Scientists* (Chicago: Educational Foundation for Nuclear Science, 1986). A collection representing various sides, though with a conservative tilt, is Ernest W. Lefever and E. Stephen Hunt, eds., *The Apocalyptic Premise: Nuclear Arms Debated* (Washington, D.C.: Ethics and Public Policy Center, 1982).

Clark and bishop's statement: Castelli, citing *Washington Post* columnist Mary McGrory, *The Bishops and the Bomb*, p. 119.

Reagan and Pontifical Academy of Sciences delegation: Castelli, *The Bishops and the Bomb*, p. 52.

For discussions of just war, cf. James Turner Johnson, *Can Modern War Be Just?* (New Haven and London: Yale University Press, 1984) and *Just War Tradition and the Restraint of War: A Moral and Historical Inquiry* (Princeton, N.J.: Princeton University Press, 1981).

Morality of intention: Catholic moral theologians have spent a good deal of energy debating the question of "intention" in deterrence. Involved in the discussion is the traditional idea that sin is in the will, not in the outward act per se. A person who has fully decided to commit murder or adultery who is then prevented from doing so by circumstances has already sinned—for sin is in the heart. Thus the problem arises: if it would be immoral to use nuclear weapons (directly against civilian population or against military targets with disproportionate civilian death and destruction), is it permitted to *possess* such weapons? Some would conclude that if the use of such weapons would be immoral, their possession is also immoral, since the intention to use them is built into the possession. Others would argue that the intention is not to use them but to deter use of nuclear weapons by others; what deters is not one's intentions, but the doubt on the part of the adversary. Others argue that in order to be effective, deterrence must entail a *conditional* willingness to use nuclear weapons—otherwise the deterrence lacks credibility. In fact, Catholic theologians and ethicists were unable to give a satisfactory account. They were afraid of following out principles absolutely and tended to take shelter by speaking of ambiguity. Part of the uncomfortableness comes from the fact that official Catholic teaching shows no sensitivity to ambiguity in its stands on sexuality and abortion. In their text the bishops seem to sidestep the whole intention issue and limit themselves to expressing their anguish in rhetorical questions.

Foreign Affairs article: McGeorge Bundy, George F. Kennan, Robert S. McNamara, Gerard Smith, "Nuclear Weapons and the Atlantic Alliance," *Foreign Affairs* 60 (1982): 753–68.

Methodist bishops' letter: The United Methodist Council of Bishops, *In Defense of Creation: The Nuclear Crisis and a Just Peace* (Nashville, Tenn.: Graded Press, 1986). The Methodist bishops issued a short pastoral letter and a "Foundation Document" comparable in length and scope to *The Challenge of Peace*. The Catholic bishops had done the opposite: the letter is the long form, but it is accompanied by a summary drawn up by the bishops.

Pope on deterrence: John Paul II, Message to U.N. Special Session, 1982, quoted in CP, 173.

Gene Sharp: *The Politics of Nonviolent Action* (Boston: Porter Sargent, 1973).

Catholic conscientious objectors in World Wars I and II: Ronald G. Musto, *The Catholic Peace Tradition* (Maryknoll, N.Y.: Orbis Books, 1986), pp. 240, 244.

Bishop Matthiessen: Castelli, *The Bishops and the Bomb*, pp. 28–30 and 57–59.

CHAPTER 3—IRRESPONSIBLE OR TOO TIMID?

Weigel: George Weigel, *Tranquillitas Ordinis: The Present Failure and Future Promise of American Catholic Thought on War and Peace* (New York: Oxford University Press, 1987). Expansion of *tranquillitas ordinis*, p. 31; Hehir's ideas as the bishops', p. 314; eight themes: stated 180–81, developed most fully pp. 356–92; criticism of *The Challenge of Peace* in chap. 9, quotes pp. 280–82; Peter Steinfels, "The Heritage Abandoned? George Weigel Explains It All," *Commonweal*, September 11, 1987, and September 25, 1987. See also David Hollenbach, "War and Peace in American Catholic Thought: A Heritage Abandoned?" *Theological Studies* 48 (1987).

Musto: Ronald G. Musto, *The Catholic Peace Tradition* (Maryknoll, N.Y.: Orbis Books, 1986).

Novak: Michael Novak, "Moral Clarity in the Nuclear Age," *National Review*, April 1, 1983. The names of those who signed Novak's statements are found in *Catholicism and Crisis*, March 1983. Others were added in subsequent issues. Members of the House of Representatives who signed were Tom Corcoran (Ill.), Henry Hyde (Ill.), Guy Molinari (N.Y.), Joe Skeen (N.M.), and

Vin Weber (Minn.), all Republicans. Page numbers here are to the version found in the *National Review*. Levels of teaching, pp. 357–58; Scripture and soldiers, p. 360; Scriptures speak of God permitting destruction of world, p. 356; nuclear weapons have not altered the fundamentals, p. 365; summary statement, p. 386.

Pacifism and just war: James Finn, "Pacifism and Just War: Either or Neither," in Murnion, *Catholics and Nuclear War*, pp. 132ff.; quotes, pp. 142–43; William V. O'Brien, "The Failure of Deterrence and the Conduct of War," in Langan and O'Brien, *The Nuclear Dilemma*, pp. 153ff., quotes, pp. 153 and 155; Gordon Zahn, "Pacifism and Just War," in Murnion, *Catholics and Nuclear War*, pp. 119ff.; quotes, pp. 119, 125, 126, 128, 130, 130–31; Quentin Quesnell, "Hermeneutical Prolegomena to a Pastoral Letter," in Charles J. Reid, Jr., ed., *Peace in a Nuclear Age*, pp. 3–19, quotes pp. 12, 14, 15, 17; Francis X. Meehan, "Nonviolence and the Bishops' Pastoral Letter: A Case for a Development of Doctrine," *Thought* 59, no. 232 (March 1984) (also in Judith Dwyer, ed., *The Catholic Bishops and Nuclear War: A Critique and Analysis of the Pastoral, "The Challenge of Peace"* [Washington, D.C.: Georgetown University Press, 1984]).

Feminist critique: Juliana Casey, *Where Is God Now: Nuclear Terror, Feminism and the Search for God* (Kansas City, Mo.: Sheed & Ward, 1987); being "only woman," p. 69; women for selling weapons, 70–71; mistrust of emotions, 55–56; summary of other patterns, p. 106.

CHAPTER 4—TOWARD A NEW AMERICAN EXPERIMENT

Choice of topics for chap. III: Archbishop Rembert Weakland, O.S.B., "Economic Justice and the American Tradition: Placing the Economic Pastoral Letter in Various Contexts" (unpublished).

CHAPTER 5—MINDING WHOSE BUSINESS? DEBATE OVER *ECONOMIC JUSTICE FOR ALL*

Conservative reactions: Buckley, David S. Broder, "Reagan Conservatives Resent Bishops' 'Untimely' Criticism," *Miami Herald*, November 11, 1984; Buchanan: *New York Times*, November 29, 1986; *USA Today*, editorial, November 15, 1984. For visceral conservative reactions, see William F. Buckley, Jr., "Vapid Thought from Bishops," Tom Bethel, "Prophecy at the Hilton," and (editorial) "The Bishops, Once More," in *National Review*, December 14, 1984. For various reactions, see "Am I My Brother's Keeper?" *Time*, November 26, 1984, pp. 81–82.

Lay Commission: William E. Simon and Michael Novak, *Toward the Future: Catholic Social Thought and the U.S. Economy—A Lay Letter* (New York: Lay Commission on Catholic Social Teaching and the U.S. Economy, 1984); William E. Simon and Michael Novak, "Liberty and Justice for All" (statement, summary, and press release). Quotes here from this statement: "defects," p. 5; wealth of some does not cause poverty of others: *Toward the Future*, p. 50; role of culture and comparisons (North to South Korea, etc.) pp. 47–48; liberty, statement, "Liberty and Justice for All," p. 4; sources not American, p. 14; no weight to U.S. economic originality, summary, p. 2; flaws in U.S. structure and "larger breakdown," summary, p. 4; bishops beyond the bounds of their authority, statement, p. 3.; partisan "middle axioms," p. 4; preferential option for the state, need to pay attention to markets, statement, pp. 8–9; see also Novak, *The Spirit of Democratic Capitalism* (New York: Simon & Schuster, 1982); *Freedom with Justice: Catholic Thought and Liberal Institutions* (New York: Harper & Row, 1984); *Will It Liberate? Questions About Liberation Theology* (New York: Paulist Press, 1986).

Silk: Leonard Silk, quoted in an editorial in *Commonweal*, November 30, 1984, p. 643. O'Leary comments: Karen Sue Smith,

"What's Become of the Pastoral?" *Commonweal*, December 18, 1987, p. 745.

Friedman: Milton Friedman, "Good Ends, Bad Means," in Gannon, *The Catholic Challenge*, pp. 99–106.

Leftist criticisms: Leonardo and Clodovis Boff, "Good News of Bishops' Economics Pastoral and Bad News Left Unmentioned," *National Catholic Reporter*, August 28, 1987, pp. 14 and 23; Lee Cormie, "The U.S. Bishops on Capitalism" (typescript, September 1985, 38 pp., unpublished): racial discrimination, pp. 22–23; William K. Tabb, "The Shoulds and the Excluded Whys: The U.S. Catholic Bishops Look at the Economy," in William K. Tabb, ed., *Churches in Struggle: Liberation Theologies and Social Change in North America* (New York: Monthly Review Press, 1986), pp. 278–90, esp. 287ff.; William E. Murnion, "The 'Preferential Option for the Poor' in *Economic Justice for All*: Theology or Ideology?" in Bernard P. Prusak, ed., *Raising the Torch of Good News: Catholic Authority and Dialogue with the World* (Lanham, Md.: University Press of America, 1988), pp. 203–37: argument on socialist principle of justice, pp. 29ff.; more inductive approach, p. 5; bishops not overtly socialist, p. 34.

"Iron Cage": Norman Birnbaum, "The Bishops in the Iron Cage: The Dilemmas of Advanced Industrial Society, in Gannon, *The Catholic Challenge*, pp. 153–78: thinking in terms of three decades ago, p. 155; Victor Ferkiss, "The Bishops' Letter and the Future," in Douglass, *The Deeper Meaning of Economic Life*, quote, p. 51.

Liberalism/Communitarianism: David Hollenbach, S.J., "Liberalism, Communitarianism and the Bishops' Pastoral Letter on the Economy," paper given at the meeting of the Society of Christian Ethics, January 18, 1987, 32 pp.; summary paragraph, p. 26. A seminal work in the discussion is Alasdair MacIntyre, *After Virtue* (Notre Dame, Ind.: University of Notre Dame Press, 1981); see also Michael J. Sandel, ed., *Liberalism and Its Critics* (New York: New York University Press, 1984).

CHAPTER 6—BRINGING IT HOME: THE LETTERS AND THE CHURCH

National Catholic Reporter poll: Karen Sue Smith, "What's Become of the Pastoral?" *Commonweal*, December 18, 1987, p. 742.

Religion and political attitudes: Stephen Hart, "Justice and Faith: How American Christians View Economic Issues" (unpublished manuscript); "The People, Press & Politics" (Los Angeles: Times-Mirror, 1987); Andrew Greeley, *American Catholics Since the Council*, chap. 3, "The Political Context"—chart constructed from information on pp. 43–44.; information on the peace pastoral pp. 93ff.; also Andrew M. Greeley, "Why the Peace Pastoral Didn't Bomb," *National Catholic Reporter*, April 12, 1985.

Implementation of letters: Catherine Inez Adelsic, "The Effort to Implement the Pastoral Letter on War and Peace," in Reid, *Peace in a Nuclear Age*; newsletters of the Office of Implementation set up after the economics pastoral; Karen Sue Smith, "What's Become of the Pastoral?" *Commonweal*, December 18, 1987; *The Pastorals on Sundays* (Chicago: Liturgy Training Publications). Two of these booklets were published in 1988. With the third booklet, due in 1989, the series will complete its coverage of the three-year Church lectionary. Peggy O'Neill, M.S.W., "Views on Nuclear Weapons and Peace in the Catholic Diocese of Richmond: Three Years Later" (Richmond, Va.: Office of Justice and Peace, Catholic Diocese of Richmond, 1986); figures on what would be required at Catholic universities in David Johnson, "Educating for Peace: Into the Mainstream," in Reid, *Peace in a Nuclear Age*; *Momentum: Journal of the National Catholic Educational Association*, December 1983; on Campaign for Human Development see several long articles by Arthur Jones, Maryclaire Dale, and Jim McManus in *National Catholic Reporter*, August 28, 1987.

Justice within the Church: salaries: *Philadelphia Inquirer*, February 14, 1988, section E; Andrew Greeley, William McManus,

Catholic Contributions: Sociology and Policy (Chicago: Thomas More Press, 1987) pp. 140ff.

Consistent ethic of life: National Conference of Catholic Bishops, "To Live in Christ Jesus: A Pastoral Reflection on the Moral Life," November 11, 1976 (Washington, D.C.: United States Catholic Conference, 1976); Joseph Cardinal Bernardin, addresses at Fordham University, December 6, 1983, Seattle University, March 2, 1986, and Saint Louis University, March 11, 1984; Francis X. Meehan, "Abortion and Nuclear War: Two Issues, One Moral Cause" (Ligouri, Mo.: Ligouri Publications, 1984); Kristin Luker, *Abortion and the Politics of Motherhood* (Berkeley: University of California Press, 1984); Ruether summary in "Abortion: Capturing the Middle Ground," *Christianity & Crisis*, July 9, 1984; Joan Chittister, "Stepping Tentatively Between Prophetism and Nationalism," *Commonweal*, August 13, 1982, pp. 427–29, quote from p. 429.; Christine Gudorf, *Cross Currents* 34, no. 4: 473–91, quote p. 490; for abortion arguments on both sides, debate between Daniel Maguire and James Burtchaell in *Commonweal*, November 20, 1987, pp. 657–80; poll data: Andrew Greeley, *American Catholics Since the Council*, chap. 5, "Sex and Authority," pp. 80–100; Frances Kissling, "A Church Divided: Catholics' Attitudes About Family Planning, Abortion and Teenage Sexuality" (Washington, D.C.: Catholics for a Free Choice, 1986); Mary E. Hunt and Frances Kissling, "The *New York Times* Ad: A Case Study in Religious Feminism," *Conscience* 8, no. 4 (July/August 1987), and Marjorie Reiley Maguire, Ph.D., "Pluralism on Abortion in the Theological Community: The Controversy Continues," *Conscience* 7, no. 1 (January/February, 1986); Maureen Fiedler, "Claiming Our Power as Women in the Midst of Political Struggle," *Conscience* 9, no. 2 (March/April 1988).

Rome and the letters: Joseph Cardinal Ratzinger and Vittorio Messori, *The Ratzinger Report: An Exclusive Interview on the State of the Church* (San Francisco: Ignatius Press, 1985), pp. 59 and 60; Charles E. Curran, *Faithful Dissent* (Kansas City, Mo.:

Sheed & Ward, 1986) contains documentation on earlier stages of the Curran case; Hunthausen affair, *National Catholic Reporter*, November 21, 1986; Kobler study, Kennedy, *Re-Imagining American Catholicism*, pp. 50ff.; AIDS controversy, several articles in *Conscience* 9, no. 1 (January/February 1988); Arthur Jones, "Vatican Document Targets Collegiality," *National Catholic Reporter*, February 19, 1988.

CHAPTER 7—FURTHER QUESTIONS

Moffit observations: Michael Moffit, "Shocks, Deadlocks, and Scorched Earth: Reaganomics and the Decline of U.S. Hegemony," *World Policy Journal* (Fall 1987), quotes pp. 557, 561.

INDEX

ABOUT THE AUTHOR

◆ ─────────────────────────────────────── ◆

Phillip Berryman was a priest in Los Angeles and Panama. Later, from 1976 to 1980, he worked for the American Friends Service Committee in Central America. From Guatemala he returned to the United States and now lives in Philadelphia with his wife and three children. He has published numerous reviews and articles in such journals as *Commonweal*, *America*, the *National Catholic Reporter*, and *Christianity and Crisis*. He is the author of *The Religious Roots of Rebellion*, *Inside Central America*, and *Liberation Theology*.